**LIBRARY
RESOURCES**

LIBRARY
RESOURCES

How to Research and Write a Paper

C. P. LEE

Jacksonville University

PRENTICE-HALL, INC., Englewood Cliffs, New Jersey

PRENTICE-HALL INTERNATIONAL, INC., *London*
PRENTICE-HALL OF AUSTRALIA, PTY. LTD., *Sydney*
PRENTICE-HALL OF CANADA, LTD., *Toronto*
PRENTICE-HALL OF INDIA PRIVATE LIMITED, *New Delhi*
PRENTICE-HALL OF JAPAN, INC., *Tokyo*

PREFACE

This manual is especially designed for students beginning college work, because they must undertake independent library research. Such students have often regarded the library as an orchard, where they wandered and tasted at pleasure; now they face it as I face a mechanic's toolbox—warily, with mingled respect and fear.

What I print here I have been saying for years. I have said it in the classroom and in the library itself, showing the reference sets and explaining their use. Alas, the pace was too fast. Haunted by vanishing class time, conscious of how much at best I must omit, I poured out lists, advice, definitions, until even the most attentive listener missed some point that, fortunately, can be preserved in print. This manual will explain, and a reader can absorb what it explains at his own speed.

The sample pages from the *Applied Science & Technology Index,* the *Education Index,* the *Essay and General Literature Index,* and the *Readers' Guide to Periodical Literature* are reproduced by permission of The H. W. Wilson Co. The Library of Congress catalog cards are reproduced by permission of the Library of Congress. The sample paper is reproduced with the kind permission of Elliot Hindman.

C. P. LEE

CONTENTS

I

Before THE LIBRARY

1. Purpose and Use of This Manual

Sometime, usually early in the freshman year, the dread words are pronounced. "Six weeks from today," the instructor decrees, "your research paper will be due." Polysyllables thunder about the room—organization, documentation, bibliography—until the student is awed, perhaps even dazed. He need not be.

He should remember that he frequently researches; he often needs an answer and decides where that answer may be found. He telephones the post office to ask for a zip code; he consults a college catalog to discover whether, for that institution's B.S. degree, a foreign language is required. Finding the answers to such questions is a familiar task; he knows where to get the answer without conscious thought.

Now he faces an expansion of what is basically the same task, but with differences that may disturb. He now seeks a series of answers that he hopes to find in print, but he does not know in what books those answers appear. He also must shape his findings for an audience other than himself. He is uneasy. The purpose of this manual is to cure that dis-ease.

To do so, the manual will make the strange familiar. Section II, INSIDE THE LIBRARY, concentrates upon the use of the reference room, where the equivalents of the zip code directory and the college catalog are stored. Here are the reference sets, distillations of every book on the library shelves, designed to provide answers quickly and easily. INSIDE THE LIBRARY explains how to decide which of these reference sets is likely to hold the answer being sought, then explains how to search the library's other books and its periodical holdings.

BEFORE THE LIBRARY, Section I, explains how to determine exactly what we want to find. If we seek the zip code for Middletown, Ohio, the question is as clear as the answer: 45042. However, most questions are hazier. Suppose we want to find out how the Battle of Gettysburg affected the course of the Civil War. What precisely do we mean? Do we mean the effect of the battle upon the armies? Upon the morale of Union and Confederate civilians? Upon Great Britain's policy towards the combatants? We must decide whether we seek one of these, several, or all. Section I, then, explains how to clarify what we are seeking, and under what headings to look. Section III, AFTER THE LIBRARY, explains how to shape what we have found so that others can understand it. In short, this manual describes the process and logic of research.

The titles of the three sections suggest that each should be read at the indicated time. Despite that implication, an inexperienced researcher should scan the entire manual before he enters the library. Why? He must have an idea of the whole task before he concentrates upon its parts. Before we learn to drive or to swim, we can watch someone driving or swimming; we can see what we should try to do. No one can "see" the process of research. We can watch while a researcher consults one book or another, occasionally scribbling a note, but we cannot see the interplay of questions and answers that decided those movements. That unseen mental interplay, that rapid series of questions and answers, is the process of research. If we cannot see it to imitate it, how can we learn it? Only by heeding a description of what takes place in a researcher's mind.

When we see the process that we are learning, we realize that its several parts are performed at the same time. A driver watches the road as he steers, as he presses the accelerator or brake. Watching a swimmer, we see him use simultaneously his arms, legs, and head. Research is a series of mental movements as synchronized as the physical movements of swimming, but a description of research will read like a sequence: step one, step two, step three. While each section of this manual emphasizes what *must* be done at the indicated time (before, inside, and after the library), these acts are interrelated. They all actually operate at once. To realize this, the reader should first scan the entire manual, then, at the indicated time, read each section for detail.

Above all, no inexperienced researcher should begin his own particular project until he has worked the exercises at the end of

Section II, which are designed to make strange reference works familiar. True, he will handle a wider range of resources than his present project will demand, but this project is not the only research problem he will have to deal with. There will be others, in other areas of knowledge. Those exercises will not only show him what he needs now, but what he will need later. Appendix I, Basic Reference Works, will suggest sources, and the Dewey Decimal and Library of Congress numbers of the sets will send him to the right reference room shelf.

2. The Subject

Although the students listen to the instructor as he explains the research paper assignment, they often do not really hear. They are mentally asking too many questions, all but one of which they will certainly voice. The questions they ask the instructor, often in this order, will be:

a. When is the paper due?
b. How long is it to be?
c. How many books must be listed in the bibliography?
d. How many footnotes must there be?

These are questions that should be voiced. Any writer must know what time and space he has been allotted. He must also know what documentation of his paper is required. Yet a prime question may remain unspoken: How can I pick a subject that will supply enough material for the number of words required? An inexperienced researcher finds it difficult to believe the problem is usually to compress. For now, he must accept on trust that if he has access to a college library, the question of finding enough material should not enter his mind as he selects his subject.

Perhaps the subject has been assigned. In that case, half his work has been done for him. Moreover, an assigned topic is a rehearsal of what he will certainly encounter later on. Few reporters are free to choose assignments; a social worker may not avoid writing a report on food stamp distribution in his county by pleading a lack of interest. The research paper assignment, whether the topic be free or imposed, is an exercise that helps us first to teach ourselves, and then to teach others what we have learned.

If a researcher chooses his own topic, he must resist the temptation to rework a previous assignment. If he succumbs, he will probably rely too heavily upon what he has already done. He will run again to familiar books, neglecting the additional sources available in a college library, the very sources the assignment is designed to acquaint him with. Such a refurbishing may deepen his knowledge, but he must also learn to extend it. The research paper is not designed to torture the student, nor to assure that the instructor earns his salary by grading yet another set of papers. The purpose of the assignment is to teach a student how to escape his own narrow frame of reference, how to consult, not just those people he can talk to, but those whose thoughts appear only in print.

If a researcher is free to choose his subject, that very freedom may be bewildering to him. How can he select a subject, when there are so many possibilities? He may find it visually. Perhaps he sees those ominous mounds of earth the fire ant builds. Where did the pest come from, and what damage does it do? He may find his subject by a combination of personal observation and print— a car's exhaust streaming blue and a newspaper report that devices can prevent automobiles from polluting the air. What are these devices, and how do they work?

If the eye suggests nothing, he may ask himself a question about his particular field of interest. If it is boxing, who was that Marquis of Queensberry who drew up a set of boxing rules? Almost immediately the subject expands. Did not boxing rules exist before? If so, what were they, and how did Queensberry's differ? If his interest is bridge, how old are playing cards? Have there always been four suits? Why are they called "suits"?

Perhaps he expects to study medicine. How old are medical schools in Western culture? What did the early ones teach? What surgical operations could a medieval doctor perform? With what tools? Did he use any anesthetic? (That suggests another paper: Who first discovered anesthesia in the modern sense?) Someone contemplating the study of law might remember a few famous trials; for example, that of Socrates. Was there a jury system of trial in the Athens of his day? If he is interested in business, he might ask himself: Who first introduced paper money? How did people carry large sums before paper money? How did they pay for their travel?

Chaucer's Wife of Bath had been "thrice to Jerusalem." Did she carry any kind of traveler's checks?

If no personal interest can be pinpointed, then a student can examine each of his college subjects. In which is he weakest? Choosing a topic related to it can strengthen the researcher's understanding of that course. *Mathematics:* How and when were Arabic numerals introduced into Europe? *Biology:* How were plants classified in Europe before Linnaeus? *Music:* Who first wrote down music in the West, and how, and what modifications in the musical alphabet have subsequently been made?

Although the topics mentioned above are related to the present, they are not purely contemporary. We play bridge today, but the suggested subject was not the latest bridge tournament. The suggested trial was that of Socrates, not that of a Black Panther. We may, and probably will, need to research a contemporary topic later on, but such topics can be found only in current periodicals, magazines, and a handful of books. Researching a contemporary subject will not teach the inexperienced researcher the standard reference sets, and these he must learn.

The subjects suggested above are also particular, not general. They are not "Banking in the Middle Ages," "Greek Law," "Medieval Medicine," "Anesthesia." No one can handle these vast subjects in less than several hundred pages. There are many books on each of these subjects; a paper on such a subject would be nothing more than an outline. Nor can a person's life or activities be treated generally in a research paper. Irving Stone's *The Agony and the Ecstasy* is about Michelangelo; it is also about six hundred pages long. Even a limited phase of Michelangelo's life may be too broad to handle. He was a painter, a sculptor, an architect, and a poet. He was too prolific in the first three arts for a research paper to discuss adequately even one of them, but since little of his poetry has survived, "Michelangelo as a Poet" can be handled in the allotted space. If the researcher's interest is painting, then Michelangelo's activity as a painter can be subdivided; for example, "Michelangelo and the Sistine Chapel." The French Revolution cannot be treated in its entirety within the given space, but the French Declaration of the Rights of Man, voted in 1789, can be. That document was modeled upon the American Declaration of Independence. Why and what did the French borrow from it, and what did they reject?

These subjects may seem so narrow that an inexperienced researcher, concerned about the possibility of insufficient material, may worry. He must remember that not only his central question must be answered, but also many secondary questions. Examples: Why, in 1789, did the French feel the need for a Declaration of the Rights of Man? How did they know the text of the American document? What did they add to their document that was not in the American text?

Secondary questions—and there will be many—must be answered as completely as the central question if the reader is to be satisfied. What is the Sistine Chapel; when was it built; who decided to employ Michelangelo to decorate it, and why; who set the subject of the paintings; how long did the work take him; how much was he paid? What numbers were used in Europe before Arabic numerals were introduced; how did Europe learn of them; when were they first used in Europe; why did the new numbers supplant the old, and how soon? What systems of plant classification did Linnaeus know; how did his system occur to him; why did he think his system superior; how soon and by what method did it supplant the old? Answering such secondary questions will so fill the assigned space of the paper that its writer is more likely to complain of insufficient space than of insufficient material.

Assigned topics are often literary, based on the reading of poems, plays, short stories, or novels. Some literary subjects treat the background of a literary work, others the work itself. "Why Shakespeare Did Not Publish His Own Plays" is a treatment of literary background. A researcher would find that no copyright law, in our sense, existed then; that therefore there were no royalties; that the plays were valuable to their owner only as long as the text was privately retained; and that as long as the plays drew audiences, their owner would keep them under lock and key. Such a paper presents no special difficulty.

A subject which treats literary texts, however, may be more involved. An instructor suggests a paper on the short stories of Poe. He has set the material for the research, but not the specific topic. Let us assume that the class has read ten selected stories. Does the instructor's suggestion mean that the rest must be read? Probably. Poe did not write so many short stories that they cannot be read in a short time. Still, asking the instructor whether he means the paper to treat only those read in class, or the whole body, will not harm. If he says all, our first task is to read the stories we do not know. What happens next?

Before we rush to the books on Poe, we must see, without outside prompting, what subjects those stories themselves suggest. We will save time if we do our own analysis. If we do not, if we read a book on Poe's short stories in the hope that its author will analyze them for us, we will be reading to select a subject, not to find an answer. Suppose we do read such a book and find a subject; overwhelmed by print, we may take what that critic says as gospel and repeat it—a passive performance that teaches us nothing. We will have learned only how to find a printed analysis of the short stories of Poe. Worse, we may collect what every available source says about Poe's stories and dump these findings into our paper as indiscriminately as we would scrape food scraps into a garbage can.

Examining the stories, we try to see if they fall into obvious categories. If they do not, we can try the simplest classifiers: where the stories happened and when. Of the well-known stories (I exclude the others to make the example clear), some have definite settings and some do not. Most settings are European: Paris, Spain, Italy, the Norwegian coast, and even more remote points. A few stories, like "The Black Cat," have settings that might be either an American or an English city. Only one, "The Gold Bug," is definitely set in America, at Charleston and at Sullivan's Island, South Carolina. "The Mystery of Marie Roget" refers to a New York murder case, but narrates a similar case that Poe places in Paris. Why did Poe so seldom set his stories in America? That is the first subject that suggests itself. We consider it, perhaps to discard it, for if Poe never recorded his reason, we can only repeat the printed speculations of others and add our own.

Continuing, we now classify the stories according to when they happened. Some are dated as "in the year 18—," within Poe's lifetime (1809–49). Others are set in the past with little indication of even the century, like "The Cask of Amontillado." Others are in the past but fixed by reference to an event, such as "The Pit and the Pendulum," which occurs during the capture of the Spanish city of Toledo by the French general Lasalle. When some take place is difficult to determine, but we can easily allot most of his stories to Poe's lifetime or to a precise time in history.

    I. Definitely set in Poe's own lifetime:
        "The Gold Bug," "The Murders in the Rue Morgue," "The Mystery of Marie Roget," "The Purloined Letter."
    II. Definitely set in a certain historical period:
        "The Pit and the Pendulum," "The Fall of the House of

Usher," "The Cask of Amontillado," "The Masque of the Red
Death."
III. Indeterminate in time:
"The Black Cat," "The Tell-Tale Heart."

What can we notice about this list? Have the stories definitely
set in his own lifetime some common characteristic? In three of
them, the Chevalier C. Auguste Dupin is one of the characters, and
a detective. In the fourth, William Legrand wrestles with a crypto-
gram, solves it, and finds a treasure. The first group, then, consists
of detective stories. Are there any detective stories in the other
lists? No. Thus we have one category set, and we can discuss it in
a paper. One possible topic is Poe's detectives. How much of his
detectives' backgrounds does Poe explain? What do we know of
the Chevalier Dupin? Does he go to the scene of the crime? Do we
know how he has trained himself in logic? How did Mr. Legrand
happen to be a trained cryptographer? Or we could write a paper
on Poe's training to write detective stories, on his knowledge of
cryptography and murders, which enabled him to invent Legrand
and Dupin.

If the assignment is to write a paper about all the stories, not
just some of them, we continue our inspection. We look at the
first category again to see if the stories in it have any other common characteristics. In the detective stories a puzzle is solved. Is that
true in any of the stories in the other two lists? Yes: both the
stories we could not place in a definite time period, "The Black
Cat" and "The Tell-Tale Heart," solve a puzzle. Is there any
difference between the detective stories and those two? Yes: those
two are confessions narrated by the criminal, whereas the detective
stories are lengthy explanations of the intellectual process by which
the detective solved the crime. In the first group, then, the emphasis
is upon reason; in "The Black Cat" and "The Tell-Tale Heart,"
the emphasis is upon the emotions of the criminal. Does that remark apply to the stories in the second group? Is the emphasis
there upon emotion, not intellect? Upon checking, we emerge with
a triumphant yes.

This hypothesis now presents itself: Poe wrote his detective stories
to stimulate the reader's mind; he wrote his other stories to move
the reader's emotions. Pursuing that assumption, we can ask ourselves: How does the storytelling technique vary between the
"intellectual" stories and the "emotional" stories? The titles them-

selves suggest further inquiries. "The Masque of the Red Death" and "The Black Cat" suggest that he may have used more color in the emotional stories. Did he?

With a topic in mind, we speed through books on Poe's short stories. We will not have to investigate every paragraph or chapter; we know what we are looking for.

We have wrestled with the subject and defined it. But before we hurry to the library, we had best remind ourselves, in writing, of the questions we shall have to answer. Writing them now, while we are still in relative ignorance of the subject, will remind us to explain them to our readers, who will be as ignorant of the subject as we are now.

Poe's Detectives

1. Who are they?
2. Where do they come from?
3. Are they educated?
4. Where were they educated?
5. How did they become interested in crime or cryptography?
6. How do they meet the narrator?
7. What is the narrator doing in South Carolina and Paris?
8. How did Poe know enough cryptography and police detection to invent the detectives?

Suppose the paper is on Napoleon's administration of his tiny kingdom of Elba, during his exile there. Some logical questions might be:

1. Where is Elba?
2. Why and when did Napoleon go there?
3. How long did he stay, and when and why did he leave?
4. What did he administer? Army? Navy? Police? Law? Economy?
5. What kind of administration did he set up?
6. How effective was it?

These preliminary questions can be very helpful, as we shall see.

3. How to Know
Under Which Headings to Look

Whether we look in an encyclopedia or in the card catalog, which lists all books in the library, we have to guess under what word or heading to look. The best way to decide the most likely headings is to imagine which university professor to ask. Which department would we visit, and the professor of which course within that department would we ask?

Which disease, we want to know, did Poe have in mind when he wrote his "The Masque of the Red Death"? A professor of American literature is more likely to tell us the story than the name of the disease which suggested it. A professor of medicine, however, might recognize the disease, either by the name Poe gives it or by its symptoms, which Poe describes. So we substitute for the professor of medicine a medical dictionary (his equivalent in print), searching its index for the headings *Red Death* or *Death, Red*.

If we want to know how Arabic numerals were introduced into Europe, a professor of the history of mathematics or a professor of Arabic history might serve. They suggest the headings *Mathematics—History* and *Arab, Arabic Civilization*. Since our question is about one branch of mathematics, *Numerals,* we add that to the list. Which shall we use first? *Numerals* is the most precise; it is a division of mathematics, as mathematics is a division of the cultural history of the Arabs. We shall probably find part of what we want in an encyclopedia under *Numerals,* but the broader headings may not be ignored. The index of a book on Arabic civilization or science, under the subdivision mathematics, may yield more detail on the subject than a six-volume history of mathematics.

Suppose the paper is on how the trial of Socrates was conducted. He was tried in Athens, which was a city state. *Socrates* suggests philosophy, *city state* suggests government and politics, and *trial* suggests law. A professor of philosophy can tell us what Socrates taught; a professor of government will know whether Athens at that time was aristocratic, oligarchic, democratic, or a mixture of those; but a professor of law, perhaps a specialist in ancient Greek law, can probably provide the exact information we require. We translate these academic gentlemen into headings:

Socrates; Athens; Philosophy, Greek
Law, Greek
Greece, Ancient
Law—History

If the subject is "Robert Penn Warren as a Nashville Agrarian," one that has probably been assigned, both a professor of modern American literature and a professor of modern American (Southern) history might be consulted. Thus the following headings are suggested:

United States—History, Modern
United States—Literature, Modern
Warren, Robert Penn
Agrarians

Which heading is the most precise? *Warren.* A discussion of Warren's career mentions that he belonged to a group at Vanderbilt called the *Fugitives,* which gives us another heading to pursue. When the researcher finds that the Nashville Agrarians were also called *Southern Agrarians,* he notes that heading as well.

Sometimes one heading is obvious, the other implied. The entry *Linnaeus* may lead to an explanation of his system without explaining the earlier ones, which the researcher seeks. A moment's reflection will determine that the subject is *Botany,* that it has a subdivision called *Classification,* and that in all probability these are the headings he should use.

Occasionally the researcher's biggest problem is finding the official name of what he seeks. Such a problem a biology major faced. He was asked to write a paper on the once common idea that while God permits disease, He has created and clearly marked a cure for each disease. (The idea lingers in common plant names: heart's ease, liverwort.) He looked in the index volumes of the general encyclopedia under *Plants.* Column after column of entries met his glazing eye until he finally analyzed the problem. To what professor would he go if a botanist failed him? A professor of philosophy or religion. Therefore, the idea he sought was not scientific, but religious or philosophical. He looked in the Hastings specialized encyclopedia, *Encyclopaedia of Religion and Ethics,* in the index, under *Plants.* Here he found far fewer entries, and one that read

Doctrine of Signatures. The name sounded descriptive of what he sought, and the text confirmed his guess.

The researcher's mind should probe the subject, analyze it, and neglect no clue. One student wrote a paper on whether the Romans flooded the Colosseum and staged naval battles there. He found a statement that such spectacles were staged in ancient Rome, though the source did not say that such battles were staged in the Colosseum. Then the source added, "These battles are called *naumachiae.*" That clue he neglected to follow, although what he sought exists under that entry in classical reference works.

Should a researcher look under every heading he can imagine without finding what he wants, he should consult the *Library of Congress List of Subject Headings,* which may suggest other possible headings.

Research is active, not passive. Half the battle is matching one's wits with those of the unknown person who, at some other time and place, cataloged or indexed what we want to know. We do not have to match our wits *against* his, for he was trying to help us. If we consider how his mind may have worked, he will succeed.

4. What Is a Bibliography?

A bibliography is simply a list of books, pamphlets, magazine articles, and newspaper stories on one subject. At least, that is the kind of bibliography that concerns us. (There are other kinds, such as an author bibliography, which is a list of what the author wrote.) We shall be writing a short, simple bibliography to attach to our paper, a list of what sources we have used. That list will send anyone who wants to check what we said, or learn more about the subject than we were able to present, to the sources we list as useful.

Note that clause: "that we list as useful." Ours will not be a list of what the local library owns on the subject, for many sources merely duplicate each other, or present an aspect of our subject we did not stress. Our list certainly excludes those books and articles listed in the bibliographies of the sources that we used, but which the local library does not own. If we did not use an item, or if we looked at it but it duplicated what we already had read, we do not list it.

We shall have to list the sources we find useful, but we cannot determine whether a source is useful until we read it. Therefore, as we begin reading every source, we write down the information that will allow us to list it if we decide we should. This information is put on bibliography cards.

5. *The Bibliography Card, 3″ x 5″*

A purist may object that any discussion of bibliography and note cards ought to be in Section II, INSIDE THE LIBRARY, since it is inside the library that these kinds of cards will be written. Granted, but when the researcher takes a pen to the library, he does so because he knows why he will need it and how it should be used. He should also understand why he is taking cards.

Why cards? Why not sheets of paper? Writing what he finds on sheets of paper may tempt him to use that material in his own paper in clumps. Inertia will overcome logic; he will fail to separate from its mates that one fact which logic would wish presented apart. Cards can be so easily shuffled, so easily rearranged, that logic may win. The cards, bibliography or note, are of no value in themselves; they are a means to an end. What they bear must be legible and accurate, but they need not be specimens of calligraphic art.

The bibliography card (3″ × 5″) is usually smaller than the note card (4″ × 6″) because the two sizes effectively separate the two sets of cards, and because the bibliography card bears little information. On it we write the name of the author, last name first, for our bibliography will be alphabetized by author's last name. Then the source's title, place and date of publication. Sometimes more information, such as a volume number and edition, must be added, but the examples below will clarify this.

This information not only allows us to list our sources without returning to the books themselves, but also, more importantly, enables us to indicate on each note card just what source that note came from. For this use, each bibliography card must be keyed. At the bottom of the first bibliography card, that card which represents the first source read, write a capital *A*. The card for source two (i.e., the second bibliography card) will be keyed *B*; the twenty-seventh, *AA*. This simple sign will be duplicated on each note card written from that source, followed by the page number. Then, if that note has to be footnoted, both source and page are known.

Figure 1 shows a bibliography card for the first source read, hence keyed *A*.

```
┌──────────────────────────────────────────────┐
│                                                │
│   Kellogg, Charles E.   The Soils That Support Us.  │
│                                                │
│   New York: The Macmillan Co., 1947.           │
│                                                │
│                                                │
│                                                │
│                                                │
│                      A.                        │
│                                                │
└──────────────────────────────────────────────┘
```

Fig. 1.   A 3″ × 5″ bibliography card.

That is for a book by one author. Other proper forms for the bibliographic entries are listed here in order to discuss them. (They are also listed for ready reference at the back of the manual, alongside the footnote forms.)

1. *A Book by One Author*
   Kellogg, Charles E. *The Soils That Support Us.* New York: The Macmillan Co., 1947.
2. *A Book by More Than One Author in More Than One Volume*
   Browne, Ray B. and Martin Light. *Critical Approaches to American Literature.* II v. New York: Thomas Y. Crowell Co., 1965.
3. *A Magazine Article*
   Lattimer, J. K., "Is Marijuana Dangerous?" *The Reporter.* XXV. August 1, 1967, pp. 127–34.
4. *An Encyclopedia Article, Signed*
   Hildebrandt, J. T. "Astronomy." *Collier's Encyclopedia,* v. 1. New York, 1962.

5. *An Encyclopedia Article, Unsigned*
"Hatchett, Charles." *New Century Cyclopedia of Names,* v. Two.
New York: Appleton-Century-Crofts, 1954.

Differences are evident here: sometimes the volume number is in
Arabic numerals, sometimes in Roman, and in the final entry the
volume number is written out. These differences occur because, in
every instance, the bibliographic entry exactly copies the source.

Other differences are determined by what the bibliographic entry
writer believes his reader knows or needs to know. For example,
the encyclopedia entries bear, not the number of volumes in the
set, but the volume in which the entry occurs; on the other hand,
the bibliography card for Browne and Light enters the number of
volumes in the set. The reason is that most readers know that
Collier's and the *New Century* are multiple volumes, and they wish
to go immediately to the volume in which the entry occurs. If a
reader does not know that these are multiple volume sets, the word
encyclopedia or *cyclopedia* in their titles hints that they may be,
and the volume number in the entry makes that hint a certainty.
The Browne and Light work bears no such word as *encyclopedia*
in its title, and will be visualized as one volume. That a second
volume exists shows the reader that the work is of a larger scope
than he supposed.

Finally, the magazine entry lists the page span; the encyclopedia
entries do not. These are listed in alphabetical order, so that page
numbers here do not speed a reader to the entry, whereas in a
magazine they do. Moreover, a reader knows the probable length
of an encyclopedia entry; he cannot know the length of a magazine
article unless the page span is listed, and that page span may help
him decide whether the article in question is likely to contain additional matter he may wish.

Some instructors and some manuals do not require the inclusion
of the publisher's name in the bibliography or in the footnote.
They argue that books cited in most papers will be modern and
printed in the United States, and that anyone wanting that book
can find its publisher in such a volume as *Books in Print.* In the
majority of cases, this assumption is undoubtedly correct. Thus if
the simpler form is permitted, the bibliographic entry looks like this:

Kellogg, Charles E. *The Soils That Support Us.* New York, 1947.

However, books printed abroad or before 1900 may be used, in
which case the publisher's name will simplify a reader's search

for it. This manual follows the fuller form, including the publisher's name for all books except current, standard sets. Out-of-print or little-known encyclopedia entries should always bear the publisher's name, and all bibliographic entries, most particularly encyclopedia entries, must bear the publication date, for page numbers and information may vary from one edition of an encyclopedia to another.

Some difficulty may be encountered in deciding the date of publication. Before copyright laws, a book usually bore its date of publication on the title page. Now the copyright date, printed on the back of the title page, often serves as the publication date, but a researcher may find there not one date but several. How is he to decide which date to use? My copy of Harold Nicholson's *The Congress of Vienna* bears these dates on the back of its title page:

> Copyright 1946 by Harold Nicholson
> Issued in 1961 by The Viking Press
> Eleventh Printing December 1967

Which date should be entered on the bibliography card? The 1946 edition will have the same text as my copy, for no revised edition is noted, but because a new publisher issued the book in 1961, the 1946 pagination will probably be different; if I were to use 1946 in a bibliography, my footnote page references would almost certainly be wrong. A reader trying to verify my quotation would find the 1946 edition, but turn in vain to the page I cite. Should I use, then, 1967? No, for that is the eleventh *printing*. The same plates set up on the linotype in 1961 have been reprinted eleven times. Any one of the eleven printings from the 1961 plates will bear the same pagination. 1961 is the date to write, for any printing of this edition will serve to check my citation.

Encyclopedias and individual books, particularly textbooks, often have an identifying element: Revised Edition, Eleventh Edition. In that case, add the identifying element to the bibliographic entry.

> Obler, Paul C. *Mirrors of Man*. Second Edition. New York: American Book Co., 1968.

A final caution: the bibliographic entry must be correct. Check the card against the source as soon as you write it, and be certain that even the spelling is correct. The spelling of encyclopedia titles can be tricky; *Britannica* is not spelled with two *t*'s and one *n*—

that set and the important *Encyclopaedia of Religion and Ethics* preserve the older spelling of that key word.

6. The Note Card, 4″ x 6″

Now the researcher begins to take notes, on larger cards, from source *A*. He has that list of questions scribbled just after the subject was determined, questions he knew he would have to answer. Reading *A*, he therefore has a good idea of what he is reading to find.

Here once more is the list of questions suggested by Linnaeus' classification of plants:

1. What were the systems Linnaeus knew before he devised his own?
2. What is his system?
3. When and how did he devise it?
4. How is it better than his predecessors'?
5. How rapidly did it spread?
6. Is it still used, unchanged?

As he reads source *A*, he finds this:

> While a student he became interested in the stamens and pistils of plants, which the microscope, invented nearly fifty years before, allowed him to study minutely. The paper he wrote on stamens and pistils helped to persuade him that plants could be classified by their sexual organs.

The notetaker now lets this run through his mind to decide whether he needs it. He does, for it helps to answer question three on his list. But he does not copy it. Instead, he runs the text through his mind again, this time translating it into his own words. Because copying it might seem quicker, he may wish to put off translating it until he begins to write. If he does this, he should be warned that he may be tempted to avoid the work of translation under the strain of composing his paper. To avoid the possibility of plagiarism, always reword the text *before* writing the note.

A glance at the doubly keyed card in Figure 2 gives the researcher

```
┌─────────────────────────────────────────────────┐
│                                                   │
│          As a student he studied under the microscope, │
│    3                                              │
│          invented almost fifty years before, the sex  │
│                                                   │
│          organs of plants, the stamens and pistils,   │
│                                                   │
│          and that study and a paper he wrote on it    │
│                                                   │
│          helped to shape his idea that plants could   │
│                                                   │
│          be classified by those organs.           │
│                                                   │
│                                                   │
│                        A381                       │
│                                                   │
│                                                   │
└─────────────────────────────────────────────────┘
```

Fig. 2.   A 4" × 6" note card.

his note, safely paraphrased in his own words, precisely where he got it, and what question it helps answer. (Note that stamens and pistils are defined as plant sex organs, since the researcher's audience may not be botanists.)

Is such meticulousness mere busywork? No; a researcher never knows when he shall have to footnote. He can never know when the information he is presently taking down will be contradicted by another source he reads later. One standard encyclopedia asserted that the original Kensington Stone—a stone found in Minnesota in 1898, purportedly carved by Vikings in 1362—was in the Smithsonian Institution in Washington, with a copy in Minnesota, while another encyclopedia, equally reputable, asserted that the original was in Minnesota, with the copy in Washington. Which authority was the researcher to believe? He must record the disagreement, which means footnoting the conflicting statements. If, as a matter of procedure, he had not noted where he found the first statement, he would have been forced to search for it again, not to find *it*, but to find *where* he found it.

By noting the sources, he may not only record a disagreement, but also solve it. As a matter of fact, both encyclopedias were correct. The original Kensington Stone was on exhibit at the Smithsonian for over a year, then returned to Minnesota, at which time a copy took its place. The dates when the two articles were written produced the contradiction.

Suppose he had consulted the *New Century Cyclopedia of Names* on the same subject, an excellent three-volume set published in 1954. He would have found:

> At first considered a forgery, it [the Kensington Stone] is now accepted as genuine by many authorities, although others, of equal repute, remain unconvinced.

He would note this neutral statement. Then he would find Erik Wahlgren in his *The Kensington Stone, a mystery solved* (Madison, Wis.: University of Wisconsin Press, 1958) concluding that "all available facts indicate that the inscription was carved in the 1880's, and probably in 1898." Again, if the researcher has keyed his notes, he can quickly establish the chronology of the two conflicting statements. He can see, by glancing at his bibliography cards, that Wahlgren's statement is the later one, and he can also note that while the earlier statement is by a compiler in an encyclopedia, the later statement is by someone who had studied the problem in particular and in depth. Both for that reason and because of the later date, he will be inclined to accept Wahlgren's statement as more probable. (There is another way to assess Wahlgren's work, which "How to Assess the Value of a Source" in Section II, INSIDE THE LIBRARY, will discuss.) Far more "facts" are disputed than a researcher is likely to realize when he begins. Even the date and place of Napoleon's birth have been debated, and with cause.

Now that the necessity of keying note cards has been established, the caution to take few notes in the source's words should be repeated. Those notes that are direct copyings must be heavily flagged by quotation marks, so that proper acknowledgment will be made. Direct quotations should be few and brief. The sources will vary in sentence structure and vocabulary, from complex, polysyllabic prose to prose that is simple in word and structure. If the notes are taken in the source's style, the paper that results will be a patchwork. It will read as though a hundred hands wrote it, not two.

There is an even more important reason for taking notes in one's own words: the notetaker will understand what he is writing, and so will his reader. No note should ever be taken that the notetaker does not understand, or that is worded in such a way that his audience will not comprehend it.

Here is a note that a math major wrote for a paper on the influence upon our system of measurement of the Babylonian system based on sixty. (We measure, for instance, hours and minutes this way.)

> It now appears that 60 was chosen for metrological reasons—the number 60 has many divisors.

Two words in that note the math major may understand, but his readers will not: *metrological* and *divisors*. They might guess the second; they are unlikely to guess the first. Metrology, the science of weights and measures, will probably be confused with meteorology, a more familiar word. This student used that note as he had written it. Had he run that information through his mind and recorded it in his own words, remembering his readers, he would have written:

> Sixty seems to have been chosen because it can be divided by so many numbers, by 2, 3, 4, 5, 6, and 10, a most convenient quality for a system of weights and measures.

That note makes quick sense.
One researcher read:

> It was while he was a medical student in the Netherlands, obsessed with an interest in botany, that the idea of a classification system for plants, analogous to that he was learning in anatomy, occurred to him.

The sentence is complex in structure, heavy in vocabulary, but the facts embedded in it can be translated as follows:

> While he was studying medicine in Holland, he wondered whether plants could be classified like animals, according to structure.

That version is probably nearer the student's own tone; certainly it is more quickly perceptible to his reader.

If a note is the opinion or the judgment of the source, that note should be marked as such on the card. The best method is to preface the note by a phrase such as "according to." Here is the extract:

> The most fruitful passages in Coleridge's criticism are those where he distinguishes method and internal interconnectedness as signs of the imagination.

The card should begin, "According to Salangar, a British critic, the most fruitful passages . . ." Moreover, unless the researcher can explain to himself and to his audience, in his own words, what the terms "method and internal interconnectedness" mean, he is not yet ready to write that note, whether he flags it as Salangar's or not.

The principles of the note card, then, are these: the notetaker must understand what the note means, he must write the note so that his audience will understand what it means, and he must be able to attribute that note to its source. Moreover, if that note expresses an opinion that is the source's, the note itself must remind the researcher that the opinion on that card is not his own.

Direct quotations should be copied sparingly, and they should be short, but if the temptation to quote is irresistible, then that note must be heavily flagged with quotation marks. The passage must be copied exactly, with any peculiarity of grammar or punctuation marked *sic* in parentheses (*sic*) to indicate that the peculiarity is not the transcriber's mistake. It is permissible to omit a part that is irrelevant, and that in no way modifies the sense of the quoted text. The signal for omission is three dots (. . .). If the three dots end a sentence, then write four (. . . .).

Finally, a card may bear a few related facts, but only a few. Otherwise that card will be a clump of information and may be used as such.

> Lillian Russell's original name was Helen Louise Leonard. She was born at Clinton, Iowa on December 4, 1861, and died at Pittsburgh June 6, 1922.

One card can hold her original name and her birth and death dates, but her marital career—she married four times—had best be noted on another.

7. *Summary of Section I*

Before going to the library, a researcher must:

1. Consider his subject. If he is free to choose, he must select his area, then narrow it until he can handle the subject within the assigned space. If the subject has been assigned, he must decide

whether his assignment is general or specific, and if it is general, narrow it until he has a specific topic to discuss.

2. Jot down the secondary questions he believes should be answered, in order that he may read his sources more actively, and in order that, when he writes his paper, he will remember what his reader will want to know.

3. Decide under which headings he should search.

4. Understand the different functions of the bibliography card and the note card, and understand how to key both kinds for maximum usefulness.

These things done, he knows what he wants to find in print and how to record it. He can now enter the library prepared.

II

Inside
THE
LIBRARY

1. What the Numbers
on a Library Book Mean

A small personal library may be a jumble. (Mine is.) An owner knows his books, what they look like, and what is in them. He may not bother to arrange them, or if he does, he may use any system. He may do it by color, all green bindings together, or all red; by size, with tall books on one shelf, shorter ones on another. He may arrange them according to literary form, devoting different shelves to fiction, biography, and poetry. In the nineteenth century prudish owners are said to have arranged libraries sexually, with male and female authors grouped on separate shelves.

Such a personal collection, larger and richer than most, was assembled by Sir Robert Cotton in the late sixteenth and early seventeenth centuries. Sir Robert collected not only books but also manuscripts, coins, and "antiquities," a label which covered such disparate items as the skeleton of a rare fish and the room in which Mary, Queen of Scots had been beheaded, which he had reassembled in his mansion. In Sir Robert's day public libraries did not exist, and personal libraries of any size were rare. Hence he generously allowed scholars, among them Ben Jonson and Francis Bacon, to use his collection in the library itself. Sometimes he allowed his books to circulate; when Sir Walter Raleigh decided to while away his imprisonment in the Tower by writing his *History of the World,* he borrowed Cotton's books.

When books are consulted or borrowed by many, some system of keeping track of them must be used. The books in Sir Robert's library were housed in fourteen cases, each case surmounted by a bust from Cotton's collection of sculptures. These busts, whether by chance or design, were of twelve Roman emperors and of two ladies connected, legally or illegally, with Roman heads of state—Cleopatra and Faustina. Sir Robert's librarian took inventory, making a separate list for the books in each of the cases, heading the list with the name of that case's bust.

When the fourteen lists were alphabetized by author's last name and combined into one, the librarian added after each title the name of the bust and the number of the shelf, to indicate where that title could be found. Such a system worked well as long as the scholar knew the name of the book he wanted, and as long as the librarian knew that book, knew that the Cotton library contained it, and knew where it was on the shelf; but as libraries became larger and public, no one person could cope with either the content or the location of a flood of books. Some more logical system of arrangement had to be devised, and several were.

The most popular system in the United States is that developed by Melvil Dewey (1851–1931). At Amherst, he was a student of mathematics. All his life he loved the logic and order of mathematics. When he saw disorder, he smelled waste. He disliked, for instance, the clumsiness of our system of weights and measures, that jumble of ounces and pints and inches, and he advocated the adoption of the metric system, a subject the Congress debates as I write. He hated the waste in conventional English spelling, the waste of time and paper and ink to write "through" and "night," when "thru" and "nite" would convey the same thought. He liked to simplify, and he practiced what he preached; christened Melville Louis Kossuth Dewey, he dropped "Louis" in his teens and "Kossuth" in his twenties, at the same time simplifying the spelling of "Melville" by dropping the final "le."

While at Amherst, he earned part of his expenses by working in the college library, and there he saw the flagrant waste of money, time, and energy which the haphazard system of library cataloging caused. Books stood unused on the shelves because those who sought what they contained did not know their titles. Dewey decided that the key to library arrangement should be *subject*. All books on the same subject should be, ideally, side by side on the shelves. To attain this goal, he first divided all learning into ten parts. (Hence the Dewey *Decimal* System.) For our purposes, it is not necessary to memorize his system, but we should understand its logic. Here are the ten divisions:

000–099 General Works
100–199 Philosophy
200–299 Religion
300–399 Social Sciences
400–499 Philology
500–599 Pure Sciences
600–699 Useful Arts
700–799 Fine Arts
800–899 Literature
900–999 History

The listing seems to run from general to particular. That is, a "general work" is something that purports to be all-encompassing, as the word *encyclopedia* suggests. "Philosophy" is more general than "religion," for several religions may share a philosophy yet differ in dogma or ritual. So far one can follow Dewey's thinking, but why is *Philology,* the study of speech and systems of speech, so low on the list? Did he think we use speech in "pure sciences" but not in "religion"? A twentieth-century mind evolving the same system would probably rank the categories differently.

No matter how arbitrarily he divided knowledge, he did divide it, then subdivide it. The subdivisions of the 300's, *Social Sciences,* were assigned as follows:

300–309 Social Science General Works
310–319 Statistics
320–329 Political Science
330–339 Economics
340–349 Law
350–359 Public Administration
360–369 Social Welfare
370–379 Education
380–389 Public Service and Utilities
390–399 Custom and Folklore

Again, we see Dewey's beliefs implicit in the sequence of his assignments. The mathematician places Statistics before political activity, Political Science; that before commercial activity, Economics; and that before Law. Traditional knowledge is relegated to the last category.

Each of these subdivisions was then further subdivided, in much the same way. 370–379, for instance, begins with:

370–371 General Works on Education

and so on. Then 371 is subdivided. 371.1, for example, is The Responsibilities and Duties of Teachers.

That is the sense of the system. To help librarians assign the correct number to a book, Dewey published, in 1876, *A Classification and Subject Index for Cataloguing and Arranging the Books and Pamphlets of a Library*. This book, widely used, has caused the number assigned to a book to be fairly uniform throughout the nation. "Fairly uniform" is perhaps an overstatement, for librarians have been ingenious in fitting into the system what we have learned since Dewey's day, and they have been ingenious in very individual ways, so that the Dewey number one librarian assigns a book may be very different from that which it bears in another library in the same town. Nowadays the Library of Congress prints the Dewey Decimal number it assigns a book on the catalog cards for that book and then sells these cards to most libraries throughout the nation, so that uniformity in numbering is encouraged. This system breeds some oddities; books on bombing planes are cataloged under "Useful Arts."

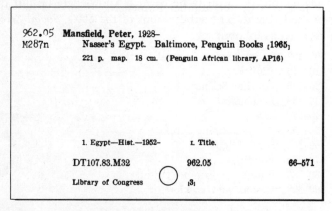

Fig. 3.   A catalog card showing the Dewey Decimal number.

Figure 3 shows a catalog card printed by the Library of Congress. A library using the Dewey Decimal System has bought that card, and a local librarian has typed, in the upper left-hand corner, two lines of numbers. The first line duplicates the printed Dewey number at the bottom of the card (962.05). The second typed line is known as the Cutter number, from the name of its inventor. The Dewey number (first line) groups together on the shelves all books *on the same subject;* the Cutter number (second line) groups together all the books with a particular Dewey number that are *by the same author.* The normal Cutter number consists of the first letter of the author's last name, two or three figures, and a small letter at the end, known as the "work letter." The Mansfield book bears the Cutter number M287n. *M* is the initial letter of Mansfield; *n* is the initial letter of Nasser, the first word of the title. (*A* and *the* are ignored.)

In three cases the Cutter number abandons its normal practice. A biography of Luther, no matter who writes it, bears a Cutter number beginning with *L.* The final small letter, or work letter, will now be the initial letter of the author's name. If Melville had written a biography of Hawthorne—the two were friends—its Cutter number, regardless of its title, would be *Hxxm;* if Hawthorne had written a biography of Melville, the Cutter number would be *Mxxh.* On biographies, then, the Cutter number performs the valuable task of ranging side by side books about the same *figure.* For precisely the same reason, criticism of an author's work, such as of Faulkner's novels, or of a composer's works, such as Wagner's *The Ring,* will bear a Cutter number formed like that of a biography. Finally, if a book is compiled by a member of an association, club, or business, that book's Cutter number will begin with the initial letter of that association, club, or firm.

As new areas of knowledge are discovered, as specialists probe more deeply into subjects, the Dewey Decimal System grows more cumbersome. Ever finer distinctions must be made to keep books on the same subject side by side. The Dewey number for the Adelman book (see Figure 4) is longer than an army serial number—016.809204. Shelving that book or copying that number on a call slip will be subject to errors. Therefore many libraries have shifted to a system devised by the Library of Congress that divides all learning into twenty branches, not ten, and uses letters as well as numbers. The Adelman book's Library of Congress classification number is Z5781, in contrast to the Dewey 016.809204. (In both systems, the Cutter number is the same—A35.)

These catalog cards show the number of the book, of course, but they also tell us much more. What do we know about the Mansfield book from that card? We know the title, publisher, and place of publication. We know that it is 221 pages long, has a map, and is eighteen centimeters high. It is one of a series: the Penguin African Library. In the card catalog there are two other cards for this same

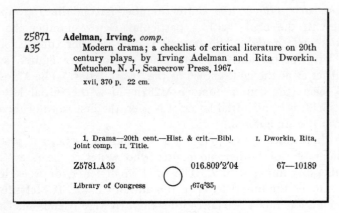

Z5871   **Adelman, Irving,** *comp.*
A35   Modern drama; a checklist of critical literature on 20th
            century plays, by Irving Adelman and Rita Dworkin.
            Metuchen, N. J., Scarecrow Press, 1967.

          xvii, 370 p. 22 cm.

          1. Drama—20th cent.—Hist. & crit.—Bibl.   I. Dworkin, Rita,
          joint comp. II. Title.

          Z5781.A35   016.809′2′04   67—10189

          Library of Congress   ₍67q²35₎

Fig. 4.   A catalog card showing Library of Congress number.

book, one under *Nasser's Egypt,* the title, another under *Egypt—
History—1952,* a subject entry. This last entry tells us where in
the card catalog we can find other books on the same subject.

The Adelman catalog card gives us the usual name of the compiler, the name of the joint compiler, the title, the publisher, and
the place of publication. We also know that it has an introduction
seventeen pages long ("xvii"), is 370 pages long, and twenty-two
centimeters high. Below, we see listed one subject entry card ("1.
Drama—20th cent.—Hist. & crit.—Bibl."), a joint compiler author
card, and a title card. All this information helps us to judge how
useful this book is likely to be. The subject entry is particularly
valuable because it gives the entry under which similar books are
cataloged.

While most items in a library are represented in the card catalog
by an author card and a title card, a moment's reflection will show
that this is not true for all; a book or pamphlet may be unsigned
and its author unknown. Nor does a card catalog contain a title
card for each item. Almost all items have titles, but many have
titles that are much alike. Imagine hundreds of entries, all pains-
takingly alphabetized, under "Introduction to . . . ."

Most libraries permit users free access to all the shelves except
those housing rare books or special collections. (Such libraries are
said to have "open stacks"; those with the opposite policy have
"closed stacks.") A researcher remembers that both the Dewey and
the Library of Congress systems are designed to shelve books on
the same subject together. When he has found one book he be-

lieves might be useful to him, he may decide to copy its call number, abandon the card catalog, and head straight for the shelf. But a shelf search should never be substituted for a catalog search. The very book we need may not be on that shelf when we scan it; it may be in circulation. The book we need may be classified some digits away from the call number of the book that led us to the shelf. Some libraries have switched from the Dewey system to the Library of Congress system without recataloging what they already owned. That library will have two separate sets of holdings on the same subject, one based on the Dewey system, the other based on the Library of Congress system. Too hasty a shelf search, without a card catalog search, will cause the researcher to overlook the second group of books.

Some libraries have one card catalog; others have two. Some list all holdings in one file; others split the file—author and title cards in one file, subject cards in another. The latter system facilitates traffic; those who know the author or title of the book they want keep out of the way of those who do not. The two-catalog system also breeds confusion. The researcher accustomed to one file may not realize (or may forget) in a new library that he is faced with two. Which system does your local library use?

2. *The Reference Room:*
Standard Sets

A card catalog lists every book in a library, and indexes list what can be found in its periodicals, but at the beginning of a search, these two keys should be ignored. Housed apart from the rest of a library's holdings are its reference works. They should always be consulted first, for they readily offer much that is not so easily available elsewhere. When we look in an encyclopedia, the text is immediately before us. We do not have to copy a call number or a volume number, then find the book or wait for it to be found. Yet these valuable reference resources, distillations of all books on the library shelves as well as of many it does not own, are little known. All students have consulted a card catalog and a periodical index, but few know much about the contents of the reference room.

One of its resources that is usually familiar is the general encyclopedia. Its scope and arrangement are known; its index volume may not be. An index volume should always be consulted before turning to a particular entry in the text. Many subjects with no title entries of their own are scattered throughout a set, and many subjects that have their own entries are also treated elsewhere. Galileo may be mentioned not only under that particular entry, but under *Astronomy* and *Inquisition* as well. Such secondary entries do not necessarily repeat the information in the first one. As we read, we should note which encyclopedia articles have bibliographies attached, that is, a list of articles in which further information may be found. We read both the text we have found and its bibliography, which tells us where to find more.

The reference room will contain several general sets; it will have the *Americana, Britannica,* and *Collier's* (Dewey–031–2; LC–AE5), at least. The order in which these should be consulted matters little, but none should be neglected. Each contains an article written by a different authority at a different time, and each article will offer a few facts the others fail to present. Some articles will be unsigned, some signed with full names, and some with initials. For the researcher's own bibliography, if for no other reason, the author's full name is needed. The list of contributors (sometimes in the index volume, sometimes in volume one) will translate these initials into names.

General encyclopedias vary in depth of coverage according to the age group they are designed to serve. The *World Book* will not treat Francis Bacon's philosophy so fully as the *Britannica,* and for precisely that reason it has its place in a reference room. The *World Book* assumes no knowledge of the subject it discusses, and it is neither technical nor verbose. It treats a subject in so small a compass that it provides an outline of it, one that a researcher can remember as he proceeds. A student writing on some phase of the French Revolution might read the *World Book* to remind himself what preceded that explosion and what happened later. He can quickly grasp an outline of the period and an explanation of some of its terminology. (For example, the term *Jacobin.*) In addition, elementary sets are profusely illustrated; the Chinese allegedly assert that one picture is worth a thousand words.

If I have to research a subject that is unfamiliar to me, for instance something in mechanics or biology, I begin with the *World Book,* continue by reading *Compton's,* and then tackle the advanced three: *Americana, Britannica,* and *Collier's.* Of these three, the last has more illustrations and, on the whole, the simplest vocabulary and syntax. Formerly, the first two exhibited different emphases. One expected, and got, more about Wordsworth in the *Britannica* than in the *Americana,* vice versa for James Fenimore Cooper. That difference has diminished in the years that the *Britannica* has been edited and published in Chicago, but it has not vanished.

When we consult a dictionary, an encyclopedia, a card catalog, or an index, we know that they are alphabetized. So familiar is this system to us that we use it almost unconsciously. We turn to the front of a dictionary if we want "aardvark," and if the eye lights on "aback," we stop; we know we have gone too far. We may be disconcerted to discover that something new, even about alphabetizing, must be learned, but we have to do so because card catalogs do not follow dictionary practice, and neither do several standard encyclopedias, for example, the *Americana.*

The two systems differ in their alphabetizing of expressions that consist of more than one word, such as *run along,* in the sense of "scram." The dictionary, which uses a letter-by-letter system, will arrange the following five words like this:

> *run, runabout, run along, run away, rune*

The word-by-word system, used in card catalogs and some encyclopedias, will arrange them like this:

> *run, run along, run away, runabout, rune*

That is, the latter system lists all expressions with *run* as the first component—*run along, run away*—before it continues with words that tack another letter onto *run* itself, such as *runabout* and *rune.* The result is that *runabout* is second in the letter-by-letter list and fourth in the word-by-word grouping.

The difference may not matter greatly when we seek an entry on an index page, for the eye, wandering up and down the entries, will find what it seeks (regardless of the system being used) if the entry is on that page. But that entry may be listed overleaf. In searching a card catalog, knowing which system it uses will be essential to finding the card we seek.

Another alphabetizing curiosity is worth attention. The letter-by-letter and the word-by-word systems act alike when they face alphabetizing a number of entries under the same word. Under *Justice* (or *Law*), for example, will be people, places, abstractions, and perhaps things. Librarians have found that researchers more often seek entries about people than about places, and more often seek entries about places than about abstractions or things. Therefore, both alphabetizing systems separate entries under the same word into these three categories, in this order: first, people; second, places; third, abstractions and things. Each category is then alphabetized within itself.

Justice, Henry W. Justice, William P.	} People
Justice Creek, W. Va. Justice Mt., Idaho Justice Mt., Wyo.	} Places
Justice, play Justice, quality	} Things and abstractions

When the general encyclopedias have been consulted, a student must be reminded that he has seen only the newest edition, whereas the older editions may be more valuable for the information he seeks. Between the eleventh edition of the *Encyclopaedia Britannica* and the present edition more than fifty active years have intervened, years that recorded two world wars and a scientific explosion. Yet the two sets are much the same in bulk; something has been omitted in the newest edition, just as something has been added, and what has been omitted may be precisely what the researcher seeks. For a subject such as "The Introduction of Arabic Numerals into Europe," the older set is much more detailed. This fuller treatment of many subjects is the reason libraries keep the older sets. Unless the subject is modern history, modern science, or technology, the older sets should be consulted as well as the new before the general encyclopedias are considered exhausted.

The English-language general encyclopedias assume that the reader is more interested in what happened in the United States or Great Britain than in Iraq, but other sets admit a much more special point of view. One such point of view is religious. Two sets of this type are the *New Catholic Encyclopedia* (Dewey–282; LC–BX841) and the *Jewish Encyclopedia* (Dewey–296.03; LC–DS102). What is Rosh Hashana? What is the doctrine of Purgatory? For the dogma, feasts, and religious figures of these two faiths, these sets are essential, but, equally important, they also discuss matters of interest to the general reader from that faith's point of view. A paper on the establishment of the missions in California or Florida, a paper on medieval philosophy, even a discussion of the rise of banking will be strengthened by reference to the *New Catholic Encyclopedia,* which will explain the Church's attitude toward interest. (Use the index volume.) While the *Jewish Encyclopedia* is more restricted in scope, much Christian belief and practice stems from the Hebraic; a paper on the Dead Sea Scrolls would have to mention the Essenes, and to ignore what the *Jewish Encyclopedia* has to say about them would be a mistake. Because these sets are so much more wide-ranging than their titles imply, a student should thumb through a volume of each set to test its range.

Two other sets, shelved nearby, are also religious, but they are interested in all faiths equally. These are the *New Schaff-Herzog Encyclopedia of Religious Knowledge* and the Hastings *Encyclopaedia of Religion and Ethics* (Dewey–203; LC–BR95; BL131). Both have index volumes. Both treat Aztec and Melanesian beliefs as fully as Jewish or Catholic or Protestant tenets, although we know far less, of course, about the first two. Any paper on comparative religion, on beliefs, on customs, must rely heavily upon these sets. Is the story of the Flood worldwide? How has Heaven or Hell been pictured by religions other than Christianity? The Hastings set should also be consulted for any subject in the humanities, since religion has affected all aspects of life. It contains much information that is difficult to find elsewhere. Read its articles on "Dress," "Food," and "Good and Evil."

A student writing on Pennsylvania Dutch hex signs learned that the "Dutch" settlers were really "Deutsche," or German. He consulted Hastings' index volume, under "hex," to find that the word means "witch" in German, and more important, to find a discussion of the old German belief in witches' powers. The student reasoned that these "Dutch" in Germany believed in witches in the eighteenth century; Germans immigrating to Pennsylvania in that century might well have used the signs superstitiously, although he found sources denying that the signs were more than decoration.

Nearby will be the *International Encyclopedia of Social Sciences* (Dewey–303; LC–H40). The "social sciences" are those areas of knowledge which, ever since the eighteenth century, have aspired to be exact sciences. They include anthropology, economics, geography, political science, psychology, sociology, and all their subdivisions. Each of these subdivisions has its own specialized reference works, but this general social science set discusses its topics for the general reader without using the jargon of some of the more specialized sets. Look up the Crusades in the *Britannica,* then in the *New Catholic Encyclopedia,* then in the *International Encyclopedia of Social Sciences.* The shift in emphasis will be apparent. This last set is more interested in cause and effect than in chronology. (Before the 1968 edition, this set was entitled simply *Encyclopedia of Social Sciences,* and each of its bound volumes actually contained two volumes, separately paged.) Though history is often termed a social science, this set does not stress it, for there have long been special sets devoted solely to this subject.

The Oxford *History of Technology* (Dewey–609; LC–T15.553), a five-volume set, concentrates upon the history of a technique: road building, the use of armor in warfare, the conversion of iron to steel. It treats chronologically man's conquest of his environment, under such chapter headings as Housing, Mining, Power, Transport; its chapters are clearly written, it has excellent illustrations, and it is a mine of information concerning the daily life of man at any period. For such subjects as how the Romans built a road, when steel was first used in bridges, or how a Venetian galley was constructed, it is an essential source, but it can also prove useful even when the subject seems farfetched. Many a literary work remarks that the medieval English stage evolved from the use of wagons for the early miracle plays; this set shows us pictures of the medieval English wagon (or wain), which was by no means what we moderns are likely to visualize.

A very special set is the *Library of Original Sources* (Dewey–080; LC–AC1.T4). Many reference works discuss the Magna Charta or the Declaration of Independence, but do not print the text of the document discussed. This set reproduces, with little comment, such political texts, as well as Harvey's essay on the circulation of the blood, the first edition of Malthus' "Essay on Population," and the like.

One set that may be present—it has been out of print for years—has a cryptic title: *The New Larned History for Ready Reference, Reading, and Research,* with a supplement. This set has a special value: the text is a skillful interweaving of quoted extracts from books. The Larned set presents research already performed, from books an individual library may not possess, or books long out of print. It is useful for any subject its date of publication does not preclude, but it must be used with discretion, since new discoveries have modified or contradicted what the Larned History reports. It is also somewhat awkward to use; it has no index volume, but is arranged like a dictionary. A little ingenuity may be required to find the right entry.

Rare is the research topic that does not involve at least one person. Major figures are easy to trace; special encyclopedias record their lives if they were artists, musicians, politicians, or the like. But suppose they were not major figures, like the man Gray mentions in his "Elegy Written in a Country Churchyard."

> Some village Hampden, that with dauntless breast
> The little Tyrant of his fields withstood;
> Some mute inglorious Milton here may rest,
> Some Cromwell guiltless of his country's blood.

Milton and Cromwell can be found by any researcher. But Hampden? Presumably he was British; therefore the most useful set is the *Dictionary of National Biography* (Dewey–920.042; LC–DA28), which is used so frequently by researchers that it is familiarly known as the *DNB*. It has supplements (which may contain the person sought) and several indexes. The American equivalent is the *Dictionary of American Biography* (Dewey–920.073; LC–E176), which also has supplements. These two sets chronicle the lives of both major and minor figures. Milton and Cromwell have their entries; there is also a full entry for Cromwell's son, Richard, who succeeded his father as Lord Protector for less than a year. What happened to that unfortunate Dr. Mudd who set John Wilkes Booth's leg? Why was Commodore Vanderbilt so called? Whenever a researcher encounters a name, and that name is British or American, these two sets will make the man and the paper come alive.

The *Dictionary of American History* and the *Album of American History* are essential sources, not only for history in the narrow sense of who landed where or fought whom, but for American clothes, furniture, methods of transport, all of which concerned every American, even Thoreau. No paper on Walden Pond or the forty-niners or the Nantucket Whalers or *Uncle Tom's Cabin* should be written without consulting these sets. The old *Harper's Cyclopedia of American History,* if it is available, is more leisurely and detailed than most modern sets can afford to be. (Its ten volumes were published in 1903.) Fuller in its discussion of political events, it lacks the treatment of general topics the other sets offer.

Near these sets will be shelved the *Handbook of American Indians*

North of Mexico, in two volumes, useful not only for information concerning the Indians themselves, their games, their clothes, their trade routes, but for many investigations of American colonial history or of the frontier.

The student interested in American history, exploration, even politics, should also consult the *Oxford Companion to Canadian History and Literature* (Dewey–810; LC–PR9106), a one-volume encyclopedia which also discusses from the Canadian view many persons and movements in American history.

This last volume is one of a series of one-volume works so useful to all students, throughout college and after, that a student should examine them in the reference room with an eye to purchasing copies of some of them for his own desk. When did Christopher Marlowe die? Who were the Muses, what were their names, and which art did each represent? When was *Huckleberry Finn* written? What did Aristotle say about the Unities; about Tragedy? What is the plot of *Antigone?* Who composed the opera "Orfeo ed Euridice"? For the quickest answer to these and countless other questions, consult the following first:

> *Oxford Companion to American History*
> *Oxford Companion to American Literature*
> *Oxford Companion to Canadian History and Literature*
> *Oxford Companion to Classical Literature*
> *Oxford Companion to English Literature*
> *Oxford Companion to French Literature*
> *Oxford Companion to Music*
> *Oxford Companion to the Theatre*

Each of these volumes will be surrounded on the shelves by larger and more extensive works on the subject each *Oxford Companion* treats. The *Oxford Companion to Classical Literature* (Dewey–913; LC–DE5), for example, will be near the *Oxford Classical Dictionary* and the *New Century Handbook,* which discuss phases of Greek and Roman life more fully than the *Companion,* while the older *Harper's Dictionary of Classical Literature and Antiquities* (1923) frequently contains more detail than the rest. Nevertheless, the *Companions* present concisely information the larger volumes ignore, and with a general audience in mind.

No tour of a reference room can mention all its holdings. We have been introduced to a few standard reference sources, those of widest usefulness. (More are listed and annotated in the Appendix.)

Hundreds of other aids exist in even the smallest college reference collection. There are general and specific literature references: *Encyclopedia of World Literature, Encyclopedia of European Literature, Cambridge History of English Literature, Ohio Books and Authors.* There are scientific encyclopedias, both general and specific: *McGraw-Hill Encyclopedia of Science and Technology,* and specific encyclopedias for biology and chemistry. Similar books exist for art: *Encyclopedia of World Art,* as well as specific encyclopedias for music, painting, and theatre. Their contents are so plainly labeled that one who needs them will consult them if he knows that they exist.

Just as the reference room is a distillation of the entire library, so the four books which follow are distillations of the reference room. They list, by subject, various reference works. They are in effect card catalogs of the reference room.

1. Barton, Mary N., comp. *Reference Books: A Brief Guide for Students and Other Users of the Library.* 6th rev. ed. Baltimore: Enoch Pratt Library, 1966.
2. Murphey, Robert W. *How and Where to Look It Up.* New York: McGraw-Hill Book Co., 1958.
3. Shores, Louis. *Basic Reference Sources: An Introduction to Materials and Methods.* Chicago: American Library Association, 1954.
4. Winchell, Constance M. *Guide to Reference Books.* 8th ed. Chicago: American Library Association, 1967.

3. The Reference Room:
Periodical and Other Indexes

After the encyclopedias, dictionaries, and standard sets have been exhausted, the researcher turns to the periodical indexes. He has waited to do so because research in periodicals is much more time-consuming than in sets. One index usually keys an entire standard set; a periodical index usually covers only one year, so that to cover twenty years means consulting twenty separate indexes.

Another time-consuming factor is that, unlike doing research with standard sets, the text is not at hand when the researcher finds an entry he wants. He must copy the periodical index entry, get the bound volume of magazines from the stacks or a microfilm of it from another part of the library, then open that volume or adjust the microfilm, all this before he can see whether his work is wasted. Here are a few tips to save time.

First, the periodical indexes are keys to what exists in print, not to what exists in any given library. Colleges of recent foundation, for example, usually possess few files of magazines for the years preceding their foundation. A researcher using a library founded in 1929 will not consult, except as a last resort, the *Readers' Guide to Periodical Literature* or any other periodical index for the years 1900–1928. Second, no college subscribes to every periodical. Somewhere in the reference room is a revolving spindle with flaps, a device that looks like a metal book and is called a "visible file." On it, alphabetized slips of paper list the periodicals to which that library subscribes. (Unfortunately, they frequently neglect to state what year the local files of that periodical begin.) The reference librarian will know the year most periodical holdings begin. He can also show the researcher the periodicals catalog, an alphabetized list by title, sometimes also by subject, of the local periodical holdings, with the volumes locally available.

Copying long lists of periodical index entries, if done indiscriminately, wastes time. Not all the entries copied will be locally available, or equally useful; we must sift as we copy. How? Suppose we are interested in the use of herbs in medicine. Which of these six entries under *Herbs* on the sample page from the *Readers' Guide* should we bother to consult?

> HERBS
>> Books. M. F. K. Fisher. New Yorker 42:226-30+ S 24 '66
>> Herbs. G. Foster. il Horticulture 44:22-5 O '66
>> Herbs. R. N. Allen. il Horticulture 44:38-9+ My '66
>> Herbs, in your garden, in your kitchen. il Changing T 20:39-40 Ap '66
>> Midsummer feast. H. S. Witty. il Flower Grower 53:36+ Ag '66
>> Practical approach to herbs. il Flower Grower 53:34-5 Ag '66
> *See also*
>> Dill
>> Garlic
>> Yarrows

534   READERS' GUIDE TO PERIODICAL LITERATURE March 1966–February 1967

HERBALS. See Botany, Medical
HERBERG, Will
 Death of God theology. por Nat R 18:7:1+,
  839-40, 884-5 Ag 9-S 6 '66
 Post-Vatican II theology. Nat R 18:421-4 My
  3 '66
 What is religious freedom? Nat R 18:1228-
  30 N 29 '66
HERBERT, Clarke L.
 They shall have music. Am Ed 2:22 O '66
HERBERT, Donald Jeffry
 Return of the wizard. il por Time 83:80 O
  7 '66
HERBICIDES
 Herbicide mixtures, a good tool for con-
  trolling weeds. G. Miller and R. Behrens.
  Suc Farm 64:34+ Mr '66
 Preemergence weed killers for corn and soy-
  beans. Suc Farm 64:90+ Mr '66
 Weeds to small grains, how to control them.
  L. W. Mitch. Suc Farm 64:37+ Mr '66
   Injurious effects
 Availability of a cationic herbicide adsorbed
  on clay minerals to cucumber seedlings.
  J. B. Weber and D. C. Scott. il Science
  152:1400-2 Je 3 '66
 Toxicity of aquatic herbicides to daphnia
  magna. D. G. Crosby and R. K. Tucker.
  bibliog il Science 154:289-91 O 14 '66
HERBS
 Books. M. F. K. Fisher. New Yorker 42:226-
  30+ S 24 '66
 Herbs. G. Foster. il Horticulture 44:22-5 O '66
 Herbs. R. N. Allen. il Horticulture 44:38-9+
  My '66
 Herbs, in your garden, in your kitchen. il
  Changing T 20:39-40 Ap '66
 Midsummer feast. H. S. Witty. il Flower
  Grower 53:36+ Ag '66
 Practical approach to herbs. il Flower Grower
  53:34-5 Ag '66
   See also
 Dill
 Garlic
 Yarrows
HERBST, Josephine
 Spain's agony; a period of exposure. Nation
  203:91-4 Jl 25 '66
HERCULANEUM
 Herculaneum. by J. J. Deiss. Review
  Time il 88:130 N 25 '66
HERCULES, incorporated
 Hercules enters tactical missile field. J. F.
  Judge. il Tech W 19:28-9 N 7 '66
HERDING of sheep. See Sheep herding
HEREDITY
 Elusive code of life. B. Commoner; J. Ken-
  drew; L. L. Whyte. il Sat R 49:71-9 O 1 '66
 Inheritance of reactivity to experimental
  manipulation in mice. N. D. Henderson.
  bibliog il Science 153:650-2 Ag 5 '66
 Inherited variations of human serum α-
  antitrypsin. F. Kueppers and A. G. Bearn.
  bibliog il Science 154:407-8 O 21 '66
 Who should bear children? F. Marley. il
  Sci N 90:537 D 24 '66
   See also
 Chromosomes
 Genetics
HEREDITY of disease
 Does it run in the family? S. G. Streshinsky.
  il Parents Mag 41:61-3+ N '66
 Genetics and the survival of the unfit. L.
  Eisenberg. il Harper 233:53-8 F '66; Reply
  with rejoinder. H. J. Muller. 232:13 Je '66
 Sex-linked anemia: a hypochromic anemia
  of mice. M. Bannerman and R. G.
  Cooper. bibliog il Science 151:581-2 F 4 '66
HEREMANS, Joseph F. See Vaerman, J. P.
  jt. auth.
HERESY
 Case of heresy? concerning Bishop Pike. il
  Newsweek 68:68 N 7 '66
 In defense of heresy. A. Towne. Christian
  Cent 84:44-7 Ja 11 '67
   See also
 Apostasy
 Inquisition
HERING, Doris
 Regional ballet, USA. See occasional issues
  of Dance magazine
HERLONG, Albert Sydney, 1909-
 Excerpt from debate. June 30, 1965. Cong Di-
  gest 45:21+ Ja '66
HERMAN, J. Clayton
 Corn late? try cold storage. Farm J 80:56T
  O '66
HERMAN, Jerry
 Sweet Sue. il Time 87:44 Ap 22 '66
HERMAN, Leon M.
 Close-up: talk with Leon M. Herman; inter-
  view. ed. by J. Berry. pors Duns R 88:8-9+
  S '66

HERMAN, Melvin. See Schreiber, F. R. jt.
  auth.
HERMENEUTICS, Biblical. See Bible—Her-
  meneutics
HERMITS
   See also
 Eccentrics and eccentricities
HERNIA
 Polyp. hernia like LBJ's not rare. Sci N
  90:393 N 12 '66
 President's surgery no small matter. F.
  Marley. Sci N 90:443 N 26 '66
HERO worship
 Hard times for heroes; D. Meredith. G.
  Astor. il Look 31:82-3 Ja 10 '67
HERODOTUS
 Dix confirms Herodotus' tales. il Sci N 90:
  426 N 19 '66
 Herodotus and the strategy and tactics of
  the invasion of Xerxes. A. Ferrill. bibliog
  f Am Hist R 72:102-15 O '66
HEROES
 Notes and comment: Meredith, Stafford, and
  Cernan. New Yorker 42:27 Je 18 '66
 On the difficulty of being a contemporary
  hero; Time essay. Time 87:32-3 Je 24 '66
 Who is a hero? and why? interview with five
  celebrities. il Mlle 63:57-9+ Jl '66
   See also
 Great men
 Hero worship
 Television heroes

   Anecdotes, facetiae, satire, etc.
 Handful of heroes. L. Rosten. il Look 30:
  24 Ja 13 '66
HEROES and lovers; story. See Silverman, R.
HEROINES in literature. See Characters in lit-
  erature
HERON, David W. and Blanchard, J. R.
 Seven league boots for the scholar? pors
  Library J 91:3601+ Ag '66
HERONS
 Egrets and herons make home near oil
  refinery; do-it-yourself bird sanctuary in
  water-conservation lagoons. il Sci N 90:
  147 S 3 '66
 No fly-by-night operation; Stone Harbor bird
  sanctuary. B. Gilbert. il Sports Illus 24:
  36-8+ Je 20 '66
HERPES simplex virus
 Partial purification and electron microscopy
  of virus in the EB-3 cell line derived from
  a Burkitt lymphoma. I. Toplin and G.
  Schidlovsky. bibliog il Science 152:1084-6
  My 20 '66
 Polysomes and protein synthesis in cells in-
  fected with a DNA virus. R. J. Sydiskis
  and B. Roizman. bibliog il Science 153:76-
  8 Jl 1 '66
 Virus: mixed infection with herpes simplex
  and simian virus 40. A. S. Rabson and
  others. bibliog il Science 151:1535-6 Mr 25
  '66
HERR, Michael
 Fort Dix: the new army game. Holiday 39:
  68-9+ Ap '66
 Museum of modern art. Holiday 40:115-18+
  D '66
HERRERA, Philip
 Eavesdropping in Harlem. Reporter 34:47-8
  My 5 '66
 —See McQuade, W. jt. ed.
HERRESHOFF, Halsey C. and Newman, J. N.
 Antlope sails indoors. pors Yachting 120:55-
  7+ D '66
 Study of sailing yachts; with biographical
  sketches. Sci Am 215:10, 60-8 bibliog (p 114)
  Ag '66
HERRINGTON, William C.
 International issues of Pacific fisheries; adap-
  tation of address. Dept State Bul 55:500-4
  O 3 '66
HERRMANN, Cyril C.
 Systems approach to city planning. Harvard
  Bsns R 44:71-80 S '66
HERSEY, M. Leonard
 Control points. See issues of Yachting
 Powerboats in competition. Yachting 119:67-
  9+ F '66
HERSH, Burton
 New twin cities. Holiday 39:50-5+ Je '66
HERSHEY, Lenore
 Sight and sound. See issues of McCall's
HERSHEY, Lewis Blaine
 Draft: an old problem; Congress takes an-
  other look; summary of testimony. June
  22, 1966. por US News 61:28-9 Jl 4 '66
 Equality does not exist; excerpts from testi-
  mony before the House armed services
  committee. Time 88:13-14 Jl 1 '66

Two are likely useless: "Herbs in your garden, in your kitchen" and "Practical approach to herbs." "Midsummer feast" is almost certainly useless, both because of its title, which indicates the use of herbs in food, and because of the name of the periodical (*Flower Grower*) in which the article appears. The two entries simply entitled "Herbs" are both in *Horticulture*. The one by Foster is three pages long (22-5); that by Allen is shorter (38-9+). If we have to choose one, we choose the longer. We have no other way of deciding which one to consult, for the title of the article is general, and so is the title of the magazine. True, *Horticulture* does suggest that the readers are more likely to find articles on growing herbs than on their use; yet we know that growers are also interested in the use of what they grow. It is unlikely that the use of herbs in medicine will be discussed in a three-page article in such a magazine, but it is possible. Shall we bother to look up these two?

We examine the other entry. It is obviously an article on books about herbs; it appears in *The New Yorker;* it is over four pages long. Short of seeking out the article, we have no way of knowing whether one of the books mentioned concerns medicinal herbs, but of all the entries, because of its length and its appearance in a periodical of general interest, it is our best bet. That entry should be copied even if all the others are rejected.

Now we look at the three "see also" entries: Dill, Garlic, Yarrows. (I had to look up the last in a dictionary; I had never heard the word before.) Suppose we already know that garlic has been used in medicine; we might turn to the entry. But before doing so, we cast a glance at the other entries on the page. (We shall probably have already encountered the precise name we seek in the standard sets, but let us suppose we have not.) There, at the very top of the page, is this entry:

HERBALS. See Botany, Medical.

The words sparkle. Alertness as we search is the key to success.

If there is one periodical index that a student is familiar with, that index is the *Readers' Guide to Periodical Literature.* He knows that it lists articles by author, title, and subject, and he is aware that for most researchers the subject entry is the most important. This periodical guide corresponds to a general encyclopedia; it is nearer to the *Americana* than the *McGraw-Hill Encyclopedia of Science and Technology.* This index has the widest subject range and the least technical articles, for it indexes magazines that appeal

226 EDUCATION INDEX

FRIENDSHIP
Friendships among students in desegregated schools. G. H. Bradley. J Negro Ed 33:90-1 Wint '64
Good judgment is impersonal judgment. R. E. Brown. Nations Sch 73:105-9 Ap '64
Operation understanding. J. Epstein. il NEA J 53:22-4 Mr '64
FRINGE benefits. See Non-wage payments
FROGS
Basic concepts in physiology: Keith Lucas and the nerve-muscle response. D. L. Smith. bibliog diags Am Biol Teach 25:610-15 D '63
Laboratory exercise: permanent microscopic preparation of the frog's tissues. S. Feldman. Am Biol Teach 26:269-70 Ap '64
Parasitism, hyperparasitism, and commensalism. A. Amaro. bibliog Am Biol Teach 26:264-5 Ap '64
Pollywogs to frogs. J. E. Hyer and M. D. Hyer. il Grade Teach 81:44+ Ap '64
Techniques and methods of recording action potentials in frog sciatic peroneal nerve preparation. H. I. Runion. bibliog il diags Am Biol Teach 25:589-97 D '63
FRONTIER and pioneer life

United States
Authenticity of the historical background of the Little house books. R. Cooper. bibliog f El Engl 40:696-702 N '63
Frederick Jackson Turner and his meaning for today. L. N. Newcomer. bibliog f Social Ed 27:244-8 My '63

Projects
Pioneer cabin. L. Mahurin. il Grade Teach 81:44 F '64
Westward ho! W. L. Herman, jr. il Grade Teach 81:27+ N '63

Units of work
Westward movement. R. Dvorak. il Grade Teach 81:60-1+ N '63
FROST, Robert
Death wish in Stopping by woods. J. Armstrong. Col Engl 25:440+ Mr '64
Kennedy speaks at Frost library dedication. J. F. Kennedy. il Wilson Lib Bul 38:317 D '63
Robert Frost, the middle ground: an analysis of Neither out far nor in deep. D. J. Lepore. Engl J 53:215-16 Mr '64
Teacher visits Robert Frost. E. B. Drew. por N Y State Ed 51:20-1 D '63
FRUIT
See also
Bananas
FRUIT flies
Small animal friends. B. J. Syrocki. il Grade Teach 81:35+ O '63
FRUSTRATION (psychology)
Aggression. A. Bandura and R. H. Walters. bibliog Nat Soc Study Ed Yrbk 62 pt 1:364-415 '63
Birth order and social reinforcer effectiveness in children. B. J. Gilmore and E. Zigler. bibliog Child Develop 35:193-200 Mr '64
Occupational values and anticipated occupational frustration of agricultural college-students. P. Glick, jr. bibliog Personnel & Guid J 42:674-9 Mr '64
Sex differences in cognitive functioning as a result of experimentally induced frustration. G. D. Yonge. bibliog J Exp Ed 32:275-80 Spr '64
Studies of reinforcement of aggression; transfer of responses to an interpersonal situation. R. H. Walters and M. Brown. bibliog Child Develop 34:563-71 S '63
FUEL
See also
Propellants
FUEL cells. See Electric batteries—Fuel cells
FULBRIGHT international exchange program. See Educational exchanges
FULBRIGHT scholars. See Scholarships and fellowships
FULL-range picture vocabulary test
Comparison of individual and group administrations of the Full-range picture vocabulary test. L. Simkins and J. Burgin. bibliog J Ed Res 57:189-92 D '63
FULLMER, Daniel W.
Daniel W. Fullmer presented 1963 Nancy C. Wimmer award. Personnel & Guid J 41:833-4 My '63
FULTON COUNTY, Georgia

Public schools
Fulton County's new services building. N. J. Aaron. Am Sch & Univ 34:K4-K8 '62

FUNCTIONS
Generating functions. N. J. Fine. bibliog Nat Council Teach Math Yrbk 28:355-67 '63
Graphical interpretation of the limit of an indeterminate function. A. Baylock. Math Teach 57:104-5 F '64
Greatest integer function. H. J. Shurlow. Math Teach 57:226-7 Ap '64
Varying usage of the concept of function. C. B. Read. Sch Sci & Math 63:726 D '63
See also
Riemann surfaces
FUNCTIONS, Trigonometrical. See Trigonometrical functions
FUNCTIONS of education. See Education—Aims and objectives
FUND for the advancement of education

Early admission to college program
Early admission to college. R. B. Ekstrom. J Ed Res 57:408-12 Ap '64
FUND raising. See Colleges and universities—Finance; Money raising campaigns
FUNDAMENTAL education
Must quality education be basic education? D. W. Robinson; S. Withers. Phi Delta Kappan 44:423-34 Je '63
FUNDS. See Alumni funds
FUNERALS
Current developments in consumer economics; the costly funeral. I. D. Satlow. Bsns Ed World 44:36 N '63
FUNG, Yu-lan
Chinese philosophy since the seventeenth century. H. C. Sun. bibliog f Ed Theory 14:54-64 Ja '64
FUNGI
Performing fungi. R. Emerson. bibliog Am Biol Teach 26:90-100 F '64
FURNACES
Case for enclosed furnaces. diag Am Sch & Univ 36:32 F '64
Heart of building pumps heat, prevent fatal attack. C. A. Jung. Am Sch Bd J 148:39-40 Ap '64
FURNITURE
Selecting furniture for college residence halls. T. M. Rehder. Am Sch & Univ 34:J5-J8 '62
See also
Lecterns
School furniture
FURNITURE, Danish
Danish furniture: tools for living. A. R. Lappin. il Sch Shop 23:22-3+ Mr '64
FUSES, Electric. See Electric fuses
FUTURE
Face of tomorrow. J. I. McCord. Am Assn Sch Adm Official Report 1963:67-74
Human future. H. Smith. Nat Assn Women Deans & Counselors J 27:36-7 O '63
See also
Forecasts
FUTURE business leaders of America
FBLA chapter 3000. J. Garbin. il Bsns Ed Forum 18:22 Ja '64
FBLA convention highlights; Dallas, June 13-15, 1963. Bsns Ed Forum 18:39 O '63
FBLA forum. See issues of Business education forum
FUTURE farmers of America
Adjusting the curriculum in a Nebraska department. R. F. Welton. il Ag Ed Mag 36:6-7 Jl '63
FFA: a service to vo-ag students. A. W. Tenney. il Am Voc J 39:15-17 Mr '64
FFA banquet may provide an avenue of communication for revitalizing the vocational agriculture image. H. E. Todd. Ag Ed Mag 35:265-6 Je '63
Future farmer as his teacher sees him. C. C. Beam. Ag Ed Mag 36:162-3 D '63
Future farmers receive top awards. il Calif Ed 1:26 D '63
Michigan FFA poultry contest keeps abreast of new technology. C. Sheppard and W. A. Householder. il Ag Ed Mag 36:133-4 Ja '64
Our graduates operate dairy farms. R. L. Mitchell. il Ag Ed Mag 36:29-30 Ag '63
Promoting better supervised farming programs. J. N. Auel. Ag Ed Mag 36:138-9 Ja '64
State F.F.A. convention: who should attend? E. Cowden. Ag Ed Mag 36:181-2 F '64
Using sociometric data in improving the FFA chapter. B. Bryant. Ag Ed Mag 36:186-7 F '64
What is an FFA boy? R. Severance, jr. Ag Ed Mag 36:68-9 S '63
FUTURE homemakers of America
FHA: an enrichment for homemaking curriculum. J. M. Barber. il Am Voc J 39:18-20 Mr '64

APPLIED SCIENCE & TECHNOLOGY INDEX 1964   365

EDDY currents—*Continued*
Three-conductor elementary Clogston coaxial transmission line; calculation, fabrication and experiment. J. M. Manley. bibliog il diags Bell System Tech J 42:2551-74 N '63
Tube testing; eddy current method. il diag Light Metal Age 22:14 Je '64

EDISON electric institute
Annual convention, 32d, Atlantic City; with abstracts of papers. Elec World 161:103-10 Je 15 '64
Annual meeting of the Purchasing stores committee, Hartford, May 11-13. Elec World 161:48+ Je 1 '64
Industrial relations round table conference, Chicago. Elec World 162:100+ O 19 '64

EDITING
Editing a scientific journal; abstract. J. B. Attrill. Chem & Ind p 201; Discussion, 201-2 F 1 '64
Technical reading, writing and editing (cont). M. H. Aronson and R. C. Nelson. Instruments & Control Systems 36:91-2 N; 73-5 D '63

EDMONTON, Alberta
See also
Airports—Edmonton, Alberta

EDUCATION
Growing picture of education. L. H. Evans and G. E. Arnstein. bibliog Automation 11:56-9+ Ap '64
See also
Education, Elementary
Engineering education
Liberal education
Medical education
Moving pictures in education
Scholarships and fellowships
Technical education
Television in education
Vocational education

Great Britain
Education: Robbins report on higher education; discussion. Roy Aeronautical Soc J 68:330-42 My '64
How sixth form English is slipping. A. J. Kirkman. Engineering 197:371 Mr 13 '64
Management education crystallises out; Lord Franks' report. Engineering 196:708 D 6 '63

United States
Texas may change its education system. Chem & Eng N 42:43 Ag 3 '64

EDUCATION, Cooperative. See Engineering education—Cooperative plan

EDUCATION, Elementary
Teaching physics in the elementary grades; science curriculum improvement study. R. Karplus. il Phys Today 17:34-8 O '64

EDUCATION, Higher
Education: Robbins report on higher education; discussion. Roy Aeronautical Soc J 68:330-42 My '64
Texas may change its education system. Chem & Eng N 42:43 Ag 3 '64

EDUCATION, Technical. See Technical education

EDUCATION and industry
When gas goes to school. il Am Gas Assn Mo 46:8-12 Je '64
See also
Engineering colleges—Relations with industry

EDUCATION and state
Administration backs education aid. Chem & Eng N 42:36 Mr 2 '64

EDUCATION of workers
See also
Vocational education

EFFICIENCY, Industrial
Automation and corporate efficiency. R. R. Eppert. Automation 11:134-9 Ap '64
Beware of creeping paralysis. W. G. Shepherd. Textile World 114:85-6 My '64
Boost productivity. il Mill & Factory 74:61-72 Je '64
Critical Paths and true productivity. S. L. Kochanski. diags Engineering 198:2-3 J1 3 '64
Easy way to control production lot routing. N. L. Enrick. diag Textile World 114:59-61 Ja '64
Efficiency of cold-reduction mills in the rolling of steel strip. R. J. Bentz and W. L. Roberts. bibliog il Iron & Steel Eng 41:101-6 Mr '64
Engineer utilization. Machine Design 35:100-2 D 19 '63; 36:83-6 Ja 2; 138-40 Ja 16; 86-8 Ja 30; 146-8 F 13 '64
Making company comparisons pay. Engineering 198:385 S 25 '64
Manufacturing efficiency; a national resource. D. L. Goldy. Automation 11:143-4 S '64

Optimizing commitment timing in procuring manufacturing equipment. A. M. Hanfmann and D. Cleinow. Automation 10:54-9 N '63
Work study and related techniques. J. E. Payne. bibliog il Naval Eng J 76:471-81 Je '64
See also
Air conditioning, Industrial
Control charts
Employment management
Factories—Lighting
Factory management
Fatigue
Foundry management
Industrial engineering
Industrial management
Industrial relations
Labor productivity
Machine shop management
Machinery, Replacement of
Mechanical handling
Mine management
Music in industry
Office management
Planning
Routing systems
Standardization
Time study

EFFICIENCY, Personal
Challenge of personal professional development. C. M. Sinnett. Res/Develop 15:37 N '64

EGG white. See Albumin

EGGS
Dry cleaning for eggs. il Engineering 196:720 D 6 '63

Preservation
Effects of ultraviolet irradiation of egg liquids on salmonella destruction and performance quality with emphasis on egg white. K. Ijichi and others. bibliog Food Tech 18:1628-32 O '64

Storage
Influence of rapid cooling and storage conditions on shell egg quality. F. R. Tarver, Jr. and R. E. Choate. bibliog Food Tech 18:1604-6 O '64

Yolks
Improvement in flow properties of egg yolk solids. R. H. Forsythe and others. bibliog il Food Tech 18:747-51 My '64

EGGS, Dried
Improvement in flow properties of egg yolk solids. R. H. Forsythe and others. bibliog il Food Tech 18:747-51 My '64
Ultraviolet absorbancy of volatiles as a measure of oxidative flavor deterioration in egg powders. O. S. Privett and others. bibliog diags Food Tech 18:1485-8 S '64

EGGS, Frozen
Liquid eggs frozen in bag. il Food Eng 36:82-4 Ag '64

EGYPT
See also subdivision Egypt under special subjects, e.g.
Geology
Hydroelectric plants
Petroleum
Petroleum industry and trade
Textile industry

Antiquities
Finally it's moving day for Egypt's Abu Simble temples. il Eng N 172:64-5 Je 18 '64
Salvaging Abu Simbel. il Engineer 218:195 Jl 31 '64

EGYPTIAN glassware. See Glassware, Egyptian

EICOSATRIENOIC acid
5,11,14-Eicosatrienoic acid in podocarpus nagi seed oil. T. Takagi. bibliog Am Oil Chem Soc J 41:516-19 Jl '64

EJECTORS
For want of a weld rod; designing and fabricating a large air ejector. D. G. Poppe. Heating-Piping 36:128 Je '64
How to specify, evaluate and operate steamjet air ejectors. R. B. Power. bibliog diag Hydrocarbon Process & Pet Refiner 43:121-6 F; 138-42 Mr; 149-52 Ap '64
Power for a salt jetslinger. il diag Elec Constr & Maint 63:98-101 Je '64
Preliminary estimates for steam-jet air ejectors. Chem Eng 71:120+ F 3 '64
Use sewage ejectors, where required. A. Koral. diags Air Cond Heat & Ven 61:75-6+ Mr '64
See also
Steam jets

ELAIDINIZATION
Elaidinization of methyl oleate with mercaptans. H. W. Kircher. bibliog Am Oil Chem Soc J 41:351-4 My '64

Reprinted from the Applied Science & Technology Index *by kind permission of The H. W. Wilson Co.*

462   ESSAY AND GENERAL LITERATURE INDEX, 1960-1964

Farmers—*Continued*

United States

Hendrix, D. B. Farmers dislike Federal farm program

In Heinsohn, A. G. ed. Anthology of conservative writing in the United States, 1932-1960 p191

Yankus, S. I think freedom is everything

In Heinsohn, A. G. ed. Anthology of conservative writing in the United States, 1932-1960 p198-200

Farming. See Agriculture

Farms

See also Family farms

Valuation

A century of land values: England and Wales

In Carus-Wilson, E. M. ed. Essays in economic history v3 p128-31

Farnham, Marynia L. Foot. See Lundberg, F. jt. auth.

Farnham, Willard

Troilus in shapes of infinite desire

In McManaway, J. G. ed. Shakespeare 400 p257-64

About Individual works
Shakespeare's Tragic frontier: the world of his final tragedies

Nemerov, H. Public services and pointing hands

In Nemerov, H. Poetry and fiction: essays p349-54

Farquhar, George

"A discourse upon comedy, in reference to the English stage. In a letter to a friend"

In Elledge, S. ed. Eighteenth-century critical essays v 1 p80-99

The recruiting officer (dramatization) See Brecht, B. Trumpets and drums

About

Loftis, J. C. Survival of the Restoration stereotypes, 1693-1710

In Loftis, J. C. Comedy and society from Congreve to Fielding p43-76

Palmer, J. L. George Farquhar

In Palmer, J. L. The comedy of manners p242-74

About Individual works
The beaux' stratagem

Palmer, J. L. George Farquhar

In Palmer, J. L. The comedy of manners p242-74

Farragut, David Glasgow

About

Welles, G. Admiral Farragut and New Orleans: pt 1-2

In Welles, G. Civil War and reconstruction p114-79

Farrell, Brian Anthony

Experience

In Chappell, V. C. ed. The philosophy of mind p23-48

Farrell, James Thomas

The author as plaintiff: testimony in a censorship case; excerpt from "Reflections at fifty"

In Downs, R. B. ed. First freedom p286-301

The league of frightened Philistines; excerpt

In Lettis, R.; McDonnell, R. F. and Morris, W. E. eds. Huck Finn and his critics p321-26

Social themes in American realism; excerpt from "Literature and morality"

In Leary, L. G. ed. American literary essays p264-70

The sun also rises; excerpt from "The league of frightened Philistines"

In Baker, C. H. ed. Ernest Hemingway: critiques of four major novels p4-6

About

Nyren, D. ed. Farrell, James Thomas

In Nyren, D. ed. A library of literary criticism p165-67

Fascism

Ebenstein, W. The cult of the state

In Ebenstein, W. ed. Great political thinkers p589-600

Ebenstein, W. Totalitarian fascism

In Ebenstein, W. Today's isms p95-122

Gentile, G. The philosophic basis of fascism

In Cooperman, D. and Walter, E. V. eds. Power and civilization p261-64

Mussolini, B. The doctrine of fascism

In Ebenstein, W. ed. Great political thinkers p612-21

Mussolini, B. The doctrine of fascism [abridged]

In Classics in Western civilization p262-68

Mussolini, B. Fascism, war, dictatorship; excerpt from "The political and social doctrine of fascism"

In Ebenstein, W. ed. Modern political thought p364-70

Parson, T. Social disintegration and fascism

In Ebenstein, W. ed. Modern political thought p370-84

Piccoli, R. Italian letter

In The Dial. A Dial miscellany p125-32

See also National socialism; Totalitarianism

Europe

Mosse, G. L. Fascism

In Mosse, G. L. The culture of western Europe: the nineteenth and twentieth centuries p341-56

Germany

Einstein, A. The eve of fascism in Germany

In Einstein, A. Einstein on peace p166-213

Italy

Abbo, J. A. Modern times: Italian Fascism, by Giuseppe Prezzolini

In Abbo, J. A. Political thought: men and ideas p369-83

Mussolini, B. The political and social doctrine of fascism

In Wishy, B. W. ed. The Western World in the twentieth century p257-68

Fashion

Beaton, C. W. H. Fashion and design; excerpt from "The glass of fashion"

In Congdon, D. ed. The thirties p397-99

by range of subject matter (*Time, Reader's Digest*) or by a narrow subject range that interests many (*Yachting, Science*). More specialized, less familiar indexes approximate the specialized encyclopedias. While the researcher might consider these indexes so specialized that he will consult them only for subjects within the narrow interest range their titles suggest, three cover a wide range of material: the *Applied Science & Technology Index,* the *Business Periodicals Index,* and the *Education Index.* A glance at the reproduced sample pages from two of these will show unexpected listings.

Magazines Listed

EDUCATION INDEX	APPLIED SCIENCE & TECHNOLOGY INDEX
Business Education World	*Air Conditioning*
Child Development	*Food Techniques*
Journal of Negro Education	*Heating and Ventilation*
Social Education	*Physics Today*

These magazines are fairly specialized, but they print, as the reproduced pages indicate, information about such unexpected subjects as Robert Frost, funerals, frontier life, and Chinese philosophy. Both *Engineer* and *Engineering News* printed articles on the preservation of an Egyptian temple from flooding; *Chemistry & Engineering News* printed a discussion of educational changes in Texas. Some of these specialized journals are in every college library; others will be in the community public library or in a specialized library nearby.

The *Essay and General Literature Index* (Dewey–016; LC–AI3) also yields information its title may mask, since many researchers imagine that "essay" means Bacon's "Of Travel" or Lamb's "Dissertation on Roast Pig." Here the word "essay" means much the same as "article," but that word does not mean that the *EGLI* duplicates the indexes to magazines. Rather, it indexes parts of books; that is, it indexes collections of articles by the same author, or articles by several authors that some editor has collected. So, under *Farms,* "A Century of Land Values: England and Wales" is one essay in a collection titled *Essays in Economic History.* (That essay is in volume three, begins on page 257, and is four pages long.) Nor does *EGLI* duplicate the card catalog; *Essays in Economic History* will have title and editor cards in the catalog but not separate cards for each essay within it. Note the range of subjects on this one page: farmers, farming, Farragut, Farquhar, fascism, fashion.

The second part of *EGLI*'s title indicates that many of its entries treat literature. If the literary entry is a person, this index first lists what he himself wrote, then what has been written about him and his literary career, then what has been written about his individual works. So, under "Farquhar, George," the index first lists his work (even an adaptation of a work), then what has been written about him as a literary figure, and last what has been written on "The Beaux' Stratagem," one of his plays.

EGLI can be useful in unexpected ways. A student writing a paper on the Icelandic saga of Burnt Njal lacked the text and found that all copies his library owned were in circulation. By consulting *EGLI,* under Icelandic sagas, he discovered long portions of the text of Burnt Njal in anthologies on the library shelves, as well as discussions of that work.

The titles of the other indexes indicate their contents so precisely that a researcher need only know that they exist to judge their value for his project. The *Art Index* catalogs art magazines and museum publications. The *Biography Index* performs a double service; it indexes both periodicals and books, even parts of books. A book's title (*Seven Representative Men*) may not reveal what biographies it contains, and the card catalog may lack an entry for some of the seven men discussed. One volume of the *Biography Index* lists, under the entry *Mesmer,* a full-length book, brief biographies in magazines, and a brief treatment in *Pioneers in Mental Health.* The last entry gives the page span (42–53) and the fact that his portrait is reproduced. The *Biological and Agricultural Index* indexes by subject only; it replaces the *Agricultural Index,* published from 1916 to 1964. Finally, the *Social Sciences and Humanities Index* should not be overlooked. It indexes (by author and subject only, not by title) many learned journals in the social sciences and humanities that the other indexes ignore, including those from other English-speaking countries. (Before 1955, when it was called the *International Index,* it also indexed such journals in other languages, but these have now been dropped.) In the *Social Sciences and Humanities Index* one may find an article printed in a United States periodical that the other indexes ignore, or an article in a Canadian or British periodical the local library owns.

The title of the *Illustration Index,* a specialized one-volume index, may not suggest how useful it is. Obviously designed to trace a picture the researcher wants, it may be used for that purpose to provide an attractive title page. (Most libraries have a machine that will reproduce any page in a matter of minutes.) In addition, since illustrations illustrate, this index may be used as a shortcut to a text. A student who had just read Eliot's "The Wasteland" was curious about Tarot cards. What were they? (Or are they? He wasn't sure.) First, what do they look like? The *Illustration Index* sent him immediately to articles on the history of the cards, illustrated by pictures of the whole pack. Since the articles were in *Hobbies,* and that magazine is indexed in the *Readers' Guide to Periodical Literature,* he could have found them there, but that search would have entailed hunting through many volumes, whereas the *Index* gave him at once the magazine, date, and page number. By using the same index, another student searching for "The Adaptation of *Uncle Tom's Cabin* as a Play" found—and found quickly—not only pictures of nineteenth century playbills advertising the drama, but a history of its adaptation and performance both in the United States and abroad.

4. The Card Catalog

What the card catalog is, how to search it, what cards each book will have in the catalog, and how to read the individual cards, previous discussions have explained. (See the index.) A summary of the essential points is listed below.

1. Find out whether the local library has one catalog or two. Most libraries have one, which alphabetizes all cards—author, title, subject—in one file, like the *Readers' Guide to Periodical Literature.* Other libraries split this catalog, alphabetizing in one file the author and title cards, and in another the subject cards. The latter system facilitates traffic; those who know the author or title of the book they want keep out of the way of those who know only the general subject. Find out which system the local library uses, and remember it.

2. Card catalogs almost always alphabetize by the word-by-word system. That means that two-word entries (like "run along") follow immediately the first component entry—"run"—and are themselves

alphabetized as a group by the first letter or letters of the second word. So cards for the following entries would be in this order:

> run, run along, run away, runabout, rune

Card catalogs, like encyclopedia indexes, usually abandon strict alphabetizing when several categories exist under the same word. In such cases, people are listed first, alphabetized under their first names; then places, alphabetized by county, country, or state; then things and abstractions, alphabetized by a defining word. So:

Justice, H̲enry P. Justice, W̲illiam P.	} People
Justice C̲reek, W. Va. Justice M̲t., Idaho	} Places
Justice, a p̲lay Justice, q̲uality	} Things and abstractions

3. In general, books in the library will be represented by at least two cards in the catalog: author and title. Subject cards may also exist. (There are none, however, for novels.) Yet a book whose author is unknown will have no author card; some books, whose titles begin with a commonplace phrase ("An Introduction to . . .") may have no title card.

A researcher who knows the author's name ought to try that first, but if he knows only the last name and not the initials, he should try the title. If he remembers both author and title imperfectly, he must try the subject entry.

4. When he finds a card, he must copy precisely the Dewey or Library of Congress number in its upper left-hand corner, and he must not omit the second line, the Cutter number.

5. When he finds any card—author, title, or subject—that represents a book on his subject, he must look at the bottom of that card to see the different subject headings that book is listed under in the catalog. These subject headings will yield additional books on the subject the student is researching. A student searching for information on fur trappers found the *American Heritage History of the Great West*. The title card for that book showed that another card for it existed in the file under "The West—History." He looked under that entry and found other, similar books. No such clue should be ignored.

6. If the library has an "open" stack policy, the researcher should resist the temptation to find a book in the card catalog, then go

to the shelves believing that every other book on that subject will be neatly ranged beside the first. What is wanted may be in circulation, or misclassified, or if the local library has changed from Dewey Decimal to Library of Congress, two widely separated sections may exist, each containing half of what he needs.

If he does go to the stacks with the call number in hand, and does not find his book in its place, he should scan the shelf to either side; some other user may have pulled it out and misplaced it.

7. A thorough study of the catalog cards will often determine the possibility and extent of a book's usefulness. Look at the description of the book on the catalog card. How many volumes? Pages? Maps? Does it have a bibliography? An introduction? Illustrations? Such clues will help winnow the books listed in the catalog, or indicate which books should be consulted first.

8. Once the book is in hand, do not waste time by leafing through it; always check its table of contents and particularly its index first. The researcher who knows what he wants can quickly see if a particular book contains the information he needs.

5. How to Assess
the Value of a Source

We all know how fast the natural sciences change. A remark about chemistry published in 1920 may be as absurd today as the remark, published in 1882, that man's physical structure could never stand a speed over sixty miles an hour. Changes in the natural sciences change the social sciences too. Spinden's correlation of the ancient Mayan calendar and ours, based upon observation of Mayan artifacts, has been superseded by the Goodman-Thompson correlation, based upon subsequent diggings, and that in turn has been challenged by another based upon the new carbon-14 process of assigning a date. At any moment, in any area, new evidence may be found. Some have long believed that the Vikings discovered the American mainland before Columbus; recent excavations in Newfoundland and the discovery of the Vinland map have increased the probability that this belief is correct. We must therefore never regard as final what a source says without considering its date of publication. Who would now consider authoritative a 1950 book on the moon?

Mein Kampf, though an important book, is no authority on history or anthropology. We do not need to investigate to know about Hitler, his bias, and his purpose in writing *Mein Kampf.* What, however, are the qualifications and bias of that Dr. James R. Spillyard whose work on Calvin we have just consulted? Is he a Ph.D. in history, or an M.D.? A Doctor of Divinity of a Calvinist or an anti-Calvinist sect? We need to know, too, whether what he says is the current general opinion of those who have studied Calvin, or whether his remarks represent a maverick's view. If he is a maverick, he may, of course, be right, or more nearly right than his opponents, as the Darwinians of the 1860's have since been proved closer to the truth than the fundamentalists who fought them. Still, we need to check what other authorities think of Dr. Spillyard's work. People are fallible; people write books. Authors can be out of date, or gullible. Ignatius Donnelly, lieutenant governor of Minnesota, member of Congress, wrote one avowed novel and three books that he regarded as nonfiction. One announced that civilization began in Atlantis, the Utopian land Plato described as having long before sunk beneath the sea; another book argues that the earth's history has been shaped by a collision with a comet in prehistoric times; the third "proves" that Bacon wrote Shakespeare's plays. It would be unwise to cite any of these three as authoritative.

The most unbelievable example of credulity that I have encountered was in a freshman paper on Freemasonry. This paper stated that Moses was a Freemason, King Solomon another. The student footnoted these remarks, as well he should. His source was *The History of Freemasonry* by the Grand Master of the San Esposito Lodge of San Esposito, California, published by the Orange Grove Press.

While our suspicions ought to be aroused by books from small, little-known publishers, a book on New England covered bridges, issued by a small press, may be by the world's authority on the subject, printed by a regional press because the book interests a regional audience. Even major publishing firms occasionally put out a book we should not trust. Not long ago, such a book, published under a major New York imprint, explained that the sun stood still for Joshua and the Red Sea parted for Moses because of a collision between Venus and Mars. The book was howled down by scientists, who called it worse names than "science fiction," but it sold well, and a copy may be on the library shelves.

To judge a source's credibility as quickly as possible, we should see what critics said about it when it appeared. We first look for the book's publication date to find when the reviews were written. (If the book has been reprinted, we want the original copyright year.) Then, under the author's name, we consult that year's volume of *Book Review Digest* in the reference room. This set not only lists representative reviews, but quotes their core statements, so that a glance gives us an idea of the critical reception it met.

To use this set successfully, remember that each volume bears a year number on its spine, say 1963. But it indexes reviews beginning with March of that year. That is to say, the 1963 volume actually contains reviews appearing from March 1, 1963 until the end of February, 1964. The explanation for this is that books published in December, 1963 were often reviewed in 1964, and that the most conscientious reviews often appear the latest. If, therefore, the copyright date of the source is 1963, and reviews do not appear in the 1963 volume, try 1964. More reviews will be listed in the *Book Review Index*, but these are not digested. We shall have to go to the periodicals themselves to see what the reviewer said. The best reviews for our purpose—the scholarly reviews that appear in highly specialized journals—will often be ignored by both these sets. To find these, a student had best consult a reference librarian for help.

6. How to Decide
Which Reference Works to Consult

These exercises will familiarize a student with the basic reference works and show him the logic of deciding which to use, and in what order.

1. Who was Belle Starr and what were her birth and death dates? Belle Starr might be British, American, Canadian, or Australian.

Since she is not a figure of major importance, her life is probably chronicled in those sets that shelter minor figures. Because we do not know her nationality, we first use the *New Century Cyclopedia of Names,* which ranges worldwide. Suppose we need a fuller account of her life. We have found that she is American; we consider the *Dictionary of American Biography* and the *National Cyclopedia of American Biography.* The latter set is not likely to be helpful; Belle Starr was a crook, and the *National Cyclopedia* prefers to chronicle the respectable. The *DAB* is willing to commemorate the shady; we try that. If it fails, then the *Biography Index* will supply biographies of her, both long and short. Use this set last, because we must leave the reference room to find the texts it lists. Be very careful using the index to the *DAB.* It indexes contributors, topics, and subjects separately.

2. What happened to Dr. Samuel A. Mudd? Find this by the same sort of reasoning. Use the *Biography Index* last.

3. What U.S. diplomatic post did Clayton Powell hold? Certainly an American. *DAB* and *National Cyclopedia.* Which gives the fuller account? What are we told in the fuller account about that diplomatic post that the other fails to mention? Is Clayton Powell in the *Americana?* Use its index volume.

4. Where is Osceola buried? Any desk dictionary that includes proper names—and most do—will list Osceola as a Seminole war chief (1804?–1838). Where to look for more? Obviously in American history sets, and certainly in the *Handbook of American Indians.* Look there; then in the *Oxford Companion to American History.* You will find a disagreement about his burial place. Which source is right, and where did you look to decide? (An atlas.) Footnote the contradiction, following the form under "Special Footnotes."

5. What effect did salt have on the European settlement of America? Consider: Humans like salt. They may even need it. Does the human body need salt? That is the sort of question the *World Book* will answer; see "Salt." We know Europeans settled first on the American coasts; obviously, they boiled sea water to get salt and, as they went inland, they must have continued for a time to get it from the coast. Then what? The Indians were already inland. They needed or liked salt too. Where did they get it? Our sources will be the *Handbook of American Indians* and those American history sets that stress background articles, the *Album of American*

History and the *Dictionary of American History*. See "Salt" in the index volumes. Don't ignore the *qv*'s, which mean "which see." Names with "Salt" in them then come to mind. Salt Lake City, Salt Springs, Salt Creek. How many such names exist in America? An atlas will tell us what and where they are, but, unless we are imaginative, we will miss "Salinas," "Saline River," and "Big Lick." The bibliographies at the end of the entries may list an article which gives exactly what we want.

6. Who introduced the log cabin into the United States? What are the major headings? Log cabin, cabin, U.S. colonial history, and colonial architecture. For the first, the *DAH*, the *Oxford Companion to American History,* and the *Album*. For a good history of colonial architecture, we shall probably have to consult the card catalog, under "Architecture—U.S.—Colonial." Again, the bibliographies at the end of the entries will help.

7. What did the Indians use obsidian for, and where did they get it?

8. Henry Rolle was an English judge during Elizabeth I's reign. What odd point of law did he settle in what curious murder case? He is English, minor, and long since dead. The *DNB*.

9. Oliver Cromwell had a son who succeeded him as Lord Protector. Where is the fullest account of his life in the reference room? *New Century Cyclopedia, Britannica, DNB*.

10. Who invented the zipper? Any who-or-what-was-first question, particularly if it is American, sends us straight to Kane's *Famous First Facts*.

11. What was the first novel written by an American to be published in the U.S.? A literary question, it is also a "first" question, and concerns an American. *Famous First Facts*. If that fails, then a detailed history of American literature: *Cambridge History of American Literature* or Spiller's *Literary History of the United States*.

12. What were the SPARS? If we have no idea, we at least know that the capital letters indicate that it is a word composed of the initial letters of words, like WAC or REA. Such a word is called an *acronym*. Desk dictionaries list the most familiar; others are in the *Acronym and Initialisms Dictionary*.

13. Who invented frozen food?

14. What are the Fulbright Grants? Desk dictionaries often help. Mine gives the Fulbright Act. We guess that the Grants must stem from the Act. Shall we look in government documents? Not if we can help it; they are complicated to find, and they are in lawyers' language. Recent editions of general encyclopedias, supplements to them, or supplements to American history sets are the best bets.

15. What source in the reference room gives the fullest account of the Moundbuilders? General encyclopedias. Do not neglect the older editions; this is the sort of subject that may have been cut to squeeze in Cape Kennedy. And, of course, *Handbook of American Indians.*

16. Where is the text of von Helmholtz's important essay on "The Conservation of Energy"? When we want a *text* of an important document, historical or scientific, the first set to consult is the *Library of Original Sources.* If it isn't available, or doesn't contain the set we want, we shall have to seek the text through the catalog.

17. Find the text of the ninety-five theses Luther nailed on the church door at Wittenberg. *Library of Original Sources.* Is it in Schaff-Herzog?

18. What is the Wallace line, and what set gives the fullest account? We don't know what it is, or for which Wallace it is named; the index volume of a general encyclopedia is the best bet. A desk dictionary may define it. Don't neglect the *DNB;* remember to check the date of his death and use the right volume.

19. How widespread is the story of the Flood? We want to know how prevalent the story is. Therefore, we do not go first to a Bible commentary, although that may help. Hastings' *Encyclopaedia of Religion and Ethics.* On any question concerning religion, custom, and the like, Hastings first, then Schaff-Herzog, then the Catholic, Jewish, Islamic encyclopedias, according to the religious affiliation of the subject.

20. What are the Fire-Walkers and where may they be found? Hastings.

21. A speaker advised his audience to "grasp the nettle" when faced with a difficulty, a reference to a speech in one of Shakespeare's

plays. Which one? When we know who wrote a line and wish to place it exactly, or quote it exactly, then we use a *concordance*, if one exists. A concordance is an alphabetized list of the words in a particular work or in all of an author's works. (Concordances exist for many major authors: Chaucer, Shakespeare, Tennyson, Joyce, Emily Dickinson. Bible concordances exist also.) Under the word, each use of it by that author or in that work is recorded, and the whole line in which that word occurs is reproduced. We look under the word in our quotation that is likely to have been least used. So we use, in this case, "nettle."

22. How many times does Shakespeare use the word "poppy"?

23. When were the first mechanical clocks devised? The first astronomical clocks? This sort of "first" question is not in *Famous First Facts;* clocks antedate 1492. Also, the question is not when the first clock appeared, but the first mechanical and astronomical clocks. So we need a detailed discussion of clockmaking. General encyclopedias will help, but since this is a question concerning man as a toolmaker, *The History of Technology* is the best bet. This set is organized chronologically. If we don't know when our inventions occurred, we have to search the chapter headings or the index in each volume.

24. How did the Romans prepare the foundation for a road?

25. Ken Kesey, contemporary novelist, was president of what movie company? The clue is contemporary novelist. *Who's Who* includes all professions; *Contemporary Authors* is pertinent and more specialized; if that fails, *Current Biography*. Glance at the other specialized biography collections as you solve this question: *American Men of Science, Who Was Who, Who's Who in Education,* and the like.

26. What is the home address of Leslie Fiedler, the American literary critic?

27. Where in the Bible can one find a reference to the "seven plagues of the seven angels"? A Bible concordance. Which word will you look under?

28. Moses knew which rock in the desert to strike for water. What was the sign by which he knew?

29. Complete the quotation that begins: "Hope springs eternal in

the human breast . . . ." When we know the quotation, or part of it, and want to find the author or the rest of the quote, we use *Bartlett's Familiar Quotations* or *Hoyt's Dictionary of Practical Quotations.* Look under "Hope" in the index and run your eye down the lines. (If we have to make a speech, and think it would be nice to introduce a quotation, we can also search for these under "Hope" or "Wisdom" or "Education." This use ought to be discouraged, as should such speeches.)

30. Who said "Guns will make us powerful; butter will only make us fat"?

31. In 1962, Irwin Ehrenpreis published volume one of a projected three-volume study of Jonathan Swift. The work—*Swift, His Works, and the Age,* v. 1—was subsequently reviewed by a critic who regretted the "absence of an index." Where and on what date was this book review published? *Book Review Digest.* That rather than the *Book Review Index* because we need the critic's remark ("the absence of an index") to identify the review we want. The *Book Review Digest* quotes the core of the reviews; the *Index* lists where they are to be found. Look at both sets to see the difference, and remember: the 1962 *Digest* volume chronicles reviews from March, 1962 to March, 1963.

32. In how many entries of the *Britannica* is Galileo mentioned?

33. Who wrote the poem beginning: "Once, in a night as black as ink"?

34. Who wrote "London, 1802"? The quotation marks hint that it isn't a book or a play.

35. A resourceful freshman found not only pictures of Tarot cards, but articles about them, when he looked in the *Illustration Index.* How many articles did he find? Caution: consider what heading to look under.

36. What is a *bodhisattva*? Where is a discussion of the philosophy the term suggests? Where a discussion of the artistic representation? Dictionary. Then Hastings. Then *Encyclopedia of World Art.*

37. Correct the following misquotation: "The cat will new and the dog will have to play." Where does the correct version of the passage occur?

38. What name is connected with the single tax? Where in the reference room is the best discussion of the tax itself? Where in the reference room is the fullest account of its chief advocate's life? List three biographies outside the reference room. *World Book* first. For sources outside the reference room, *Biography Index*.

39. Where is the Abbey Theatre? Anything about the theatre or drama sends us first to the *Oxford Companion to the Theatre*.

40. What was the title of the first play presented by the Mormons after they had moved from Illinois to Salt Lake City? Again, a play. But what shall we look under?

41. How many reference works on guns are listed in Murphey's *How and Where To Look It Up*? How many on lace? On watches and clocks?

42. Who gave Theseus a ball of string, why, and how did he reward her? Theseus sounds like a Greek name. *Oxford Companion to Classical Literature,* or *Oxford Classical Dictionary*.

43. Who was the *choregus*? Rather obviously a classical word.

44. What was the name of Antigone's sister?

45. In Yeats' poem "Leda and the Swan," Leda is seduced by a Greek god in the form of a swan. Which god was he?

46. *The Redskins* is an American novel dealing with absentee landlordism in upper New York state in the 1840's. Who wrote it, and when was it published? *Oxford Companion to American Literature*.

47. Name the first novel by the American Negro author of a short story collection entitled *Uncle Tom's Children*.

48. Bronson Alcott's daughter wrote a fictional account of her father's experimental Utopian community. What is the title of the book containing this account, and when was the book published?

49. At one time, "The Testament of Cresseid" was attributed to Chaucer. Who actually wrote the poem? *Oxford Companion to English Literature*.

50. Michael Drayton was an English poet. What were his dates? Where will we find an account of his life? Where a discussion of his works? *Oxford Companion to English Literature, DNB, Cambridge History of English Literature*.

51. According to Alexander Pope's testimony, how old was he when he wrote his pastorals?

52. Who published a collection of choral pieces entitled *Scherzi Musical* and in what year? *Oxford Companion to Music.*

53. In what year did Moritz Stoehr build his quarter-tone piano? *Oxford Companion to Music.* For more on piano construction, look under "Pianoforte." For more detail, *Grove's Dictionary of Music and Musicians,* and for much more, *Music Index.*

54. What is the subject of Juvenal's sixth satire? Which of Juvenal's satires did Dr. Samuel Johnson imitate in what poem? You may need two works here: *Oxford Companion to Classical Literature* and *Oxford Companion to English Literature.*

55. Cicero mentions the *exactio ostiorum,* a Roman tax imposed in Cilicia, Syria, and other provinces. Upon what was this tax levied? *Harper's Dictionary of Classical Literature and Antiquities.* Whenever we need to know an exact detail of Greek or Roman life, this work is the most likely source. Try the phrase, then the second word.

56. Who originated Method Acting?

57. To what work by what classical author does the title of Wilfred Owen's poem, "Dulce et Decorum est," allude?

58. We want material for a paper on Flannery O'Connor's novels and short stories. She is so contemporary that not much material will be in the reference room, but we can gather a good bibliography there. *Essay and General Literature Index* will list discussions of her work. *Biography Index* will list discussions of her life, which will probably comment on her work as well. *Short Story Explication* will list discussions of particular short stories.

59. We want material for a paper on Jackson Pollock's painting. He is too contemporary for many of the standard art encyclopedias, though the more recent will contain discussions. The *Art Index* of art magazines and museum and gallery publications will help.

60. We want material for a paper on what devices prevent factories, incinerators, or cars from polluting the air. This is a subject of wide interest; popular articles will appear in the *Readers' Guide.* The *Applied Science & Technology Index* will list more technical and detailed articles.

61. We want material for a paper on the use of computers in

business. That is of general interest, so the *Readers' Guide* will be helpful. Also the *Business Periodicals Index* and the *Applied Science & Technology Index.*

62. We want material for a paper on the fire ant and how it affects agriculture. *Readers' Guide, Agricultural Index,* and *Applied Science & Technology Index.*

63. For a paper on the recent effect of Indian music on Western music, which indexes? *Music Index, Essay and General Literature Index.*

64. For a paper on Mennonite education? *Education Index, International Index, Essay and General Literature Index.*

65. What was the *gabelle,* and when was it abolished? Desk dictionary first.

66. What is a *haiku?* Quote one. Find it without leaving the reference room. Desk dictionary first.

67. Chateaubriand published a prose epic named after a North American Indian tribe. What is the name of the work, and how long did he stay in America? *Oxford Companion to French Literature.*

68. Contrast the articles on "Evangeline" in the *Oxford Companion to American Literature* and the *Oxford Companion to Canadian History and Literature.*

69. Contrast the articles on the Hudson's Bay Company in the same two works.

70. What great dramatist parodied the use of the *deus ex machina?* Two choices: *Oxford Companion to Classical Literature* and *Oxford Companion to the Theatre.* In which do you find it quicker?

III

After
THE
LIBRARY

1. Audience and Organization

A student writer often visualizes his instructor as his audience. Why not? The instructor assigned the paper; the instructor will grade it. But the instructor, unlike the general reader, will have discussed the paper's subject with its writer, will have seen the outline, will, in short, have absorbed something of the subject before he reads the paper's first line. To address the instructor, then, is to write as though continuing a conversation, whereas the writer must learn to write as though beginning one. He should therefore visualize his classmates as his audience—intelligent, but with little information about, or little interest in, his subject. He should write for what has been called "an intelligent ignoramus."

Therefore the writer should make sure that he uses words his audience will understand, avoiding words that are erudite, specialized, or hazy. He must also feed his audience his information at a pace it can handle. His sentence structure may be complex, for a reader has the benefit of eye as well as ear, but the writer must remember that the reader lacks any previous discussion of the subject, and lacks, too, those gestures and facial expressions that stress or modify what is said. The Golden Rule of writing is to write *for* the audience rather than *at* it. Every student has picked up a textbook that fails to follow this principle, and in despair has bought one of those digests of textbooks—or rather translations—that every college bookstore stocks. What we dislike in others we should not imitate.

The reader of a paper must be able to grasp easily not only the words, the sentence structure of that paper, but its logical form. A writer must choose the logical form most appropriate to his material, announce that form to his reader, and follow it. The method of organization shapes the writer's material; its announcement to the reader provides him with a compass as he ventures into the text.

What, then, are the major methods of organization which a writer must consider? There are four: Time (Chronology), Space, Cause and Effect, Comparison and Contrast.

The most obvious method of organizing a paper is by Time—first this happened, then this, then that. This is the simplest method, yet to follow it strictly may produce a list. Scholars have access to a card-index of the life of Horace Walpole, in which they can find a day-by-day account of what he wrote, ate, bought on that particular day. Such a list is designed, not for reading, but for further research. A researcher wishing to trace Horace Walpole's interest in the Berry sisters will use it to trace the development of that friendship; another may use it for a paper on the eating habits of an eighteenth-century English gentleman. A paper organized solely by time will be as jerky and fluctuating as a dictionary.

When we organize by Space, we may start at the center—perhaps describing a city—then move out. We may start at the top and move down, as for a description of a person, or move from left to right. This method is most useful in describing a city, or a college campus, or a car, but it may be used, in combination with another organizing principle, in such a paper as "Water Pollution in Florida," to treat first North Florida, then Central Florida, then South Florida.

Many papers are organized chiefly according to Cause and Effect. Such a paper might treat how Shakespeare's knowledge that boys would portray his women influenced his writing of love scenes. That the Elizabethans used boys for women's parts is the Cause; the result (or Effect) is the substitution of words for physical action in the love scenes Shakespeare wrote. The paper explaining the publication of his plays might also be organized by Cause and Effect. Plays were valuable property. Printed, that property ceased to be his. Therefore, as long as they were valuable, he took steps to keep them in manuscript form, and to keep those manuscripts safe. Why did so-and-so do such-and-such? What he did is the Effect; why he did it is the Cause.

Cause and Effect often means Causes and Effects; either may be plural, or both. If plural, they must be arranged in some order: from most important to least important, or vice versa. A good scheme is to arrange causes in order of increasing importance, so that the final, most important cause will linger in the reader's mind as he studies the effects. If causes are presented from least to most important, then effects may follow the same scheme.

Comparison and Contrast are often used to organize a paper. A comparison or contrast of two short stories or two novels requires this method. Yet it is often suitable for material that could also be organized by Cause and Effect. One paper treated the dismal failure of Sheridan's *The Rivals* on opening night (January 17, 1775), his rapid rewriting of it, and its successful restaging eleven days after its first performance. This writer chose to present his material by Cause and Effect: the failure caused the revision, and the revision caused the play's success. He could have presented the same material with Comparison and Contrast. He could have examined the two versions of the play, spotlighting in his paper what Sheridan left untouched, and what he changed in the scenes he rewrote. However, this particular student believed the audience's reaction to the two texts as significant as the differences in the texts themselves; he therefore chose to focus upon that reaction, and so properly chose Cause and Effect.

No matter which of the four methods of organization is chosen to govern generally the entire paper, other methods will (and should) be used to control parts of it. A paper on a battle may well employ Time: "At dawn the firing began. By noon . . ." Yet it will also, within the time units, employ the method of Space: "At dawn, when the firing began, Meade's left flank . . ." Then Meade's center, then Meade's right. Comparison and Contrast may govern other bits: "While Meade's troops were fresh, Lee's army had marched all night." And surely no discussions of the battle of Gettysburg would end without some statement of its effect: "The battle of Gettysburg marked the turning point of the Civil War. After that, the Confederate fortunes ebbed." Such a paper might end with a brief statement of why they ebbed: Confederate hopes of invading the North dashed, low morale—Cause and Effect. Traces, then, of several methods of organization will be used in the same paper, and properly, but the writer should choose as his prime method the one that will best control its bulk.

Once the writer has chosen his principal method of organization, he must select his strategy. Shall the items that form the proof, or evidence, be stated before the general conclusion they seem to prove; or shall the general conclusion be stated first, then the evidence? In more technical language, shall the paper move from particular to general, or from general to particular? Shall the details of the battle be presented before its importance, or vice versa? The advantage of stating the general first is that the reader is more likely to follow the particular with interest; he can see the significance of those particulars as he reads. He knows why that battle is worth reading about. "Leonardo da Vinci, known to us chiefly as a painter, was one of the most versatile men of his age." That generalization enables the reader to follow a discussion of da Vinci's accomplishments as scientist, sculptor, musician, and engineer.

The reverse method, particular to general, is used when the particulars alone are certain to hold the interest of the reader. Frequently an essay will use this strategy to catch the reader's attention, then turn to general before particular.

> On July 6, 1535, the ex-chancellor of the realm walked up a short flight of steps and addressed the man waiting for him at the top. "Pluck up thy spirits, man, and be not afraid to do thy office. My neck is very short. Take heed therefore thou strike not awry. . . ." Then, blindfolded by a piece of linen cloth that he himself had brought, he carefully placed his neck upon the block. Four hundred years later, in 1935, the Pope proclaimed him a saint. What brought Sir Thomas More to the scaffold, and why has he been canonized?

2. Outlining

The final outline is a blueprint of the writer's paper. If he has followed this manual's suggestions, that final outline will be easy to write, for he will have already outlined his material at least twice: once when he jotted down that list of questions before entering the library, and a second time when he chose his chief method of organization.

Outlining is for the writer's use, not the reader's. (How many essays are published with a preliminary outline?) Yet, for the writer's sake, it should be in sentence form, so he can be sure that what he is saying, and how he is saying it, are crystal clear to himself. He should first write a short, clear statement of the central idea he wishes to impress upon his reader.

Here are two actual thesis sentences and two outlines submitted to an instructor. (They are by students who had not followed the procedures this manual suggests.) One student wrote:

> The purpose of this paper is to give the reader a concept of what Ayn Rand's views are and how she expresses them in her books.

That will not serve. Views of what?

> *Revised:*
> The purpose of this paper is to give the reader a concept of what Miss Rand's views are on morality and how she expresses them in her books.

Here is the outline submitted.

I. Ayn Rand
   A. Childhood
   B. Mrs. Frank O'Connor
   C. Literary Career
II. Ayn Rand Views the Problem
III. Objectivism
IV. Ayn Rand's References to History

A glance at that outline shows that it is not an outline of the problem the thesis sentence treats. I and IV are useless; II and III are the core. Ayn Rand views the problem of morality; Ayn Rand finds and announces her own solution, Objectivism. If her childhood or marriage caused her to question the ideas of others on morality, then that belongs as a subdivision under II. If she searched history for ideas of morality, or to support her own, that belongs under II.

I. Ayn Rand Views the Problem of Morality
   A. As a child she doubts the accepted view
   B. As a married woman, she searches for an accepted system of morality
      1. in the writings of her contemporaries
      2. in history

II. Ayn Rand States Her Own System, Objectivism
   A. In her novels
      1. *We, the Living*
      2. *The Fountainhead*
      3. *Atlas Shrugged*

B. In her nonfiction
  1. *The Virtue of Selfishness*
  2. *For the New Intellectual*

Here is another student sentence and outline:

The ideas of the Southern Agrarian movement influenced the poetry of Robert Penn Warren.

I. Warren's Early Life
  A. Economic turmoil
II. Joins Agrarians
  A. Not inner member
  B. Agrarianism declines
III. Influence on Poetry
  A. *Thirty-Six Poems*
  B. *Promises*
  C. *You, Emperors, and Others*
IV. Conclusion

While the thesis sentence itself seems clear, it has one ambiguity: "influenced." Did Warren write in agreement with those ideas or in reaction against them? To indicate this the sentence must be revised. Then the sentence may need limiting. Are all the ideas of the Agrarians in his poems?

The major ideas of the Southern Agrarian movement are represented and endorsed in the poetry of Robert Penn Warren.

The outline submitted is illogical, to phrase the case mildly. When we split something, we expect it to fall into at least two parts. Yet I has an A, but no B. II has an A and a B, but upon examination the two do not seem related. What have "A. Not inner member" and "B. Agrarianism declines" to do with each other? Do these subdivisions together suggest "II. Joins Agrarians"? A seems to fit, but not B. I and II are likely to be useless in furthering the thesis sentence; III is the core.

Forced to revise that outline, the student jotted down these questions:

I. How did Warren learn from the Agrarians?
II. What were the ideas of the Agrarians?
III. Which of these did he represent in his poetry and in what poems?

His reading had told him that Warren was a Southerner, that he went to Vanderbilt University as an undergraduate, that at Vanderbilt he met the group, that they published a manifesto of their ideas in 1930 in *I'll Take My Stand.* He restated his thesis and subdivided his part I.

Robert Penn Warren's Poems
as an Expression of Southern Agrarian Ideas

Thesis: The major ideas of the Southern Agrarians are represented and endorsed in the poetry of Robert Penn Warren.

  I. Warren as an Agrarian at Vanderbilt
     A. An undergraduate at Vanderbilt, he meets a group of fellow students and faculty with like backgrounds and interests.
        1. They were Southern.
        2. They were literary.
        3. They were rebels.
           a. against the Thomas Nelson Page and United Daughters of the Confederacy idea of the South.
           b. against industrialization of the South.
     B. They published their work in:
        1. a magazine, the *Fugitive.*
        2. a collective manifesto, *I'll Take My Stand.*

Now he faced his II and III:

   II What were the ideas of the Agrarians?
  III. Which of these did he represent in his poetry and in what poems?

He first tried it this way:

   II. The ideas expressed in *I'll Take My Stand* (1930) which Warren represents in his poetry are:
       A. That man is a part of nature, not outside it, or superior to it.
       B. That in a modern, urban society he forgets this, and so cannot see himself whole.
       C. That individual man needs to acknowledge the insights of his ancestors to see himself as a product of his past as well as a part of nature now.
  III. Warren represents these three ideas in the following poems:
       A. He shows man as a part of nature, not superior to it, in the following poems:
          1. "Kentucky Mountain Farm"
          2. "Calendar"
          3. "Croesus in Autumn"
       B. He shows that in the modern, urban culture man forgets he is a part of nature, and so cannot see himself whole, in the following poems:

        1. Poem A.
        2. Poem B.
        3. Poem C.
    C. Agrarian idea three
        1. Poem A.
        2. Poem B.
        3. Poem C.

He considered that outline; it is logical, but it has a fault. To follow it means that each idea explained in part II must be repeated in III, or the reader will forget the argument. But to repeat the idea risks wearying the reader with a twice-told tale. The writer therefore sought a solution to the difficulty. He saw that he could incorporate II and III; he could present the idea, then the evidence at once. He chose to do so. Here is his final outline, with its title and thesis sentence.

Robert Penn Warren's Poems
as an Expression of Southern Agrarian Ideas

Thesis: The major ideas of the Southern Agrarians are represented and endorsed in Robert Penn Warren's poetry.

  I. Warren Joins the Agrarians
    A. An undergraduate at Vanderbilt, he meets a group of fellow students and faculty members with like backgrounds and interests.
        1. They were Southern.
        2. They were literary.
        3. They were rebels.
           a. against the Thomas Nelson Page and United Daughters of the Confederacy idea of the South.
           b. against industrialization of the South.
    B. They published their work in:
        1. a magazine, the *Fugitive*.
        2. a book, *I'll Take My Stand* (1930).
 II. Three chief ideas proclaimed in that book are represented in Warren's poetry.
    A. While man considers himself superior to nature and acts as though he were, he is in reality a part of it.
        1. Statement of this in *I'll Take My Stand*.
        2. Statement of this in Warren's poetry.
           a. "Kentucky Mountain Farm"
           b. "Calendar"
           c. "Croesus in Autumn"
    B. Idea two
        1. Statement in *I'll Take My Stand*.

2. Statement of this in Warren's poetry.
   a. Poem A
   b. Poem B
   c. Poem C
C. Idea three
   1. Statement of this in *I'll Take My Stand.*
   2. Statement of this in Warren's poetry.
      a. Poem A
      b. Poem B
      c. Poem C

He was now ready to write his paper.

3. *Alpha and Omega:*
The Beginning and the End

Just as the first minute of a speech is all-important—it is the only minute that everyone will be listening—so the first paragraph of a paper must capture the attention of the reader and convince him that what the paper is saying is worth his time. Many freshman beginnings fail in one of two ways: they do not capture the audience's attention, or they do not suggest what method of organization is being used.

Suppose that the subject is "The Contributions of Alchemy to Chemistry," and that the first paragraph reads:

> Alchemy is the transmutation of metals. The Greeks believed that the permutation of metals was implicit in Nature. Paracelsus said that each metal had its affinity in the planets. The sun controlled gold.

Granted that the grammar is impeccable, and that the facts are correct, this beginning fails. Why? It is jargon, impenetrable to all but those who already know about alchemy, and obviously alien to the writer himself. This dutiful bird dog has docilely brought his find to dump at his master's feet. How about this next paragraph?

> The science of alchemy was very important. Many people believed in it at the time. But it turned out that it did not succeed, and

many people were disappointed in it. However, it did some good, because the alchemists discovered many things we now know. This paper will attempt to list some of them.

That is a very poor beginning, but at least a human being is talking to other human beings. Yet he is saying little, and he says that little hazily. Look at the first two sentences: does he mean that alchemy was important because "many people believed in it at the time" or are we to suspend interest in its importance until we find in sentence four that "it discovered many things we now know"? And note that weak "will attempt," probably prophetic, since it implies failure.

Version three:

> Alchemy was the medieval science that tried to turn lesser metals to gold. There were many alchemists all over Europe and in the Near East. Although they failed to manufacture gold, their interest in what matter is and how it might be changed influenced others, the first chemists. Chemistry owes to alchemy many of its techniques, some of its equipment, and many of its terms. These contributions of alchemy to chemistry this paper will discuss.

This is a straightforward, businesslike beginning. The writer obviously understands what he is saying; he also states it clearly to his reader, and hints that he is using Cause and Effect as his method of organization. Indeed, the next to last sentence hints that he will discuss the effect of alchemy upon chemical techniques, then upon chemical equipment, then chemical terms. The writer of the first paragraph bowed his head and allowed his material to clobber him; the second mumbled what he remembered in his sleep. Writer Three is remembering his audience. However, straightforward as his paragraph is, he has not bothered to try to interest his reader. He starts bluntly: "Alchemy was the medieval science that tried to turn lesser metals to gold." So it was, but does the reader care?

A really effective introduction must attract a jaded reader's attention. One way is to put some meat on those bones. Let us rewrite it, keeping the skeleton and filling it out with what that writer already knew.

> In the Middle Ages, philosophers set the scientists the task of creating wealth by turning baser metals into gold. Dutifully, and probably greedily, the scientists boiled, baked, turned solids into gases, and gases into solids. They did not succeed in producing gold. But their interest in the nature of substances, and their invention

of tools and techniques for their search, stimulated a science that has created a wealth far more valuable to us than gold: chemistry. The world could limp along without gold, but it would crawl without plastics, synthetic textiles, synthetic leather, synthetic rubber, the new medicines and the new metals created by chemistry.

That is a better beginning than the third because it takes the trouble to stimulate the reader's interest. The writer is visualizing his reader and talking to him. The phrase "dutifully, and probably greedily," the verbs *boiled, baked, limp, crawl,* all imply that a mind is commenting on the facts presented. That beginning deserves praise.

Here are three beginning paragraphs for a paper on "How Arabic Numerals Were Introduced into Europe."

The first:

> Arabic numerals first appeared in Europe in the twelfth century. They had been introduced by the Arabs into Spain. The Arabs learned about them from the Hindus. From Spain, they spread throughout the rest of Europe.

The second:

> Arabic numerals are very important. Without them we would not be able to divide or multiply or subtract as quickly as we do. But they were not introduced into Europe until the twelfth century, after the Arabs, who had learned about them from the Hindus, had brought them into Europe by conquering Spain. Even after Arabic numbers were introduced, they were suspect, because they were easier to alter than the Roman numbers then in use.

The second is much better. Note the two vast improvements: this writer tells us quickly that something we take for granted we did not always have, and reminds us what a fix we would be in if we multiplied in Roman numerals. He creates a shadow scene: ourselves struggling to multiply CXIV by XXXVI. But he could have dramatized the scene he suggests by writing:

> In the year MCMLXIX John Doe sits down to complete his income tax form. He has earned V̄MMMCCCXXIX dollars; MDCCCLVI dollars have been withheld. If, according to the tax tables, he owes MMCCCLIX dollars, how much more must he pay? To solve even this simple problem, John Doe will translate the cumbersome Roman numerals into Arabic. Yet until the eleventh century, he had no alternative to the difficult operations Roman numerals entail. Arabic numerals, which make possible quick calculations, by hand,

by adding machine, by computer, were unknown in Europe until
the twelfth century. Even after they had been introduced by mer-
chants and scholars who had learned their use from the Moors in
Spain, they were regarded with suspicion. Were they not of enemy
origin, enemies of both the true religion and the state? Besides,
could they not be altered by medieval check-raisers more easily than
their Roman equivalents? Yet the newcomers were so obviously
useful that by the fourteenth century, the European business world
had accepted them, although Papal accounts were still kept in
Roman numerals.

That is an excellent introduction: it dramatizes the importance
of the subject in a way that will touch every reader, and also sum-
marizes what the paper will contain.

The paper must have an intelligent ending; it may not simply
stop. No sane driver enters the garage at full speed, then slams on
the brakes. Just as we should not begin the paper with "This paper
will attempt," so we must not end with "Thus we see," although
in essence that is the correct technique. Our case complete, we draw
breath and rewrite part of what we said in the beginning paragraph.
We remind the reader of what we promised to tell him in the opening paragraph, and we show him that we have kept that promise.
The ending may be short. These are examples of the simplest way
to end:

> Without the speed and accuracy of Arabic numerals, modern tech-
> nology would be impossible. A world without slide rules, without
> adding machines, without computers, might be a more leisurely
> world, but it would be a world far less comfortable physically than
> the one we know.

> Although alchemy has long been discredited, the search for gold did
> cause a new way of looking at nature, new tools and new techniques
> that have exploited nature for the benefit of man.

> Karl von Linne's system has been the basis of botanical classifica-
> tion ever since. Exchange of information about plants and exchange
> of information concerning experiments with plants have affected
> what we eat and wear and such studies as genetics as well. Mendel
> used plants to study heredity; his description of his experiments,
> published obscurely, could be verified by others because of the work
> Karl von Linne had performed.

No subject will interest every reader. "The Molecular Structure
of Sugar" is likely to enthrall a very small circle indeed, but such
technical papers are not the usual student task. He is to find in-

formation, to understand it, and to explain what he has found and understood to as wide an audience as he can command. If he searches for the connection between his subject and his contemporaries, he will find it. In trying to find such a connection, he practices a technique that will serve him well. No salesman begins his spiel with "Webster's Dictionary defines" or "According to Aristotle." Hamburger stands, even the cheapest, spice their meat with mustard, pickle, or catsup. We should pay no less attention to pleasing our customer's brain than the hamburger stand pays to pleasing his belly.

4. How to Avoid Plagiarizing:
What to Credit and How

A student who copies from another's examination paper is well aware that he is cheating, that cheating is wrong, and that he will be punished if caught. He may not know that he is also plagiarizing (the word *plagiarism* derives from the Latin for "kidnapping"), and if he knew, he probably would not care.

Yet a student who would not copy another student's paper will sometimes copy bits from printed sources, link them, and then claim this borrowed finery as his own. He assumes, as careless researchers often assume, that print is impersonal; he argues that any reader is free to borrow what he reads. Where, indeed, did the printed author get his material if not from earlier printed works? Perhaps he did, but probably he has properly acknowledged his debt.

Suppose that we are writing a paper on Napoleon at Waterloo. We must believe, since so many witnesses attest it, that Napoleon lost the battle. For the same reason, we must accept that he lost it on June 18, 1815. These are facts so commonly available and so undisputed that when we lift them from a page we need not footnote; listing the source in the bibliography will be sufficient acknowledgment. If the source writes, "Napoleon lost the battle of Waterloo on June 18, 1815," we can lift both the fact and the words. No one would censure us for reproducing that sentence exactly, without quotation marks, for the diction is so natural that any writer of English can claim it as his own. Suppose, however, that we copy that same information phrased in an unusual way. "From the first charge of the French against the British, at 11:30 a.m., on June 18, 1815, the issue of the battle was in doubt until late that evening, when the last unavailing charge of the French Old Guard convinced Napoleon that he had lost." These facts, also readily available, would not need to be set in quotation marks and footnoted, except that here an unusual phraseology, not straightforward or commonplace, marks the diction as the source's, not the student's. Acknowledgment that the diction is another's must be made, and it must be made in a footnote, for even if we write in the text "As J. W. Haskins, in his *Military Strategy at Waterloo,* remarks, 'From the first charge of the French . . .'," we shall still have to footnote to give the edition and the page.

Every instructor has encountered borrowed phrases, if not sentences, that protrude above student prose like little lava cones. Here is a paragraph from a student paper on "How *The Arabian Nights* Became Known in Europe."

> The next translation, the first reliable edition, was by Edward W. Lane, an Arabic scholar, in 1840. Lane believed that a number of incidents in the tales occurred in the period 768–808, but some of the circumstances cannot be dated earlier than the fifteenth century. This translation of *The Arabian Nights* was put out monthly by Lane, keeping the readers anxious and interested for the next tale to come out.

Which sentence did that student really compose?

This student did realize, in fact, that he owed his source something; he footnoted the passage, without any quotation marks, citing the biography of Lane in the *Dictionary of National Biography,* the famous *DNB.* Even though the writer footnotes a passage to give credit for the facts, a mere footnote does not assign credit to the source for the diction.

Moreover, he was guilty of even graver negligence, for he had borrowed judgments. He borrowed two: that the Lane edition was the first reliable version of the tales, and that Lane's belief that the tales reflect the late eighth and early ninth centuries is wrong. He should have avoided borrowing the diction and acknowledged borrowing the judgments.

The next translation, in 1840, was by an Arabic scholar, Edward W. Lane. His biographer in the *Dictionary of National Biography* calls this translation the first reliable edition. While Lane himself believed that the tales reflect historic happenings of the late eighth and ninth centuries, his biographer points out that "some of the circumstances" can be no earlier than the fifteenth century.

Why these revisions? They avoid borrowing the diction, which is undistinguished, and therefore not worth quoting; they credit the borrowed judgments far more effectively than a mere footnote. Why is the phrase "some of the circumstances" in quotation marks? Because the writer does not know what that slippery word *circumstances* means here. Historic happenings mentioned? Language?

Does that revision need a footnote? No; the set is standard, the entry in that set is obviously *Lane,* and the entry is so short that any interested reader can find quickly the quoted words without footnote help. But such a case is rare.

Judgments are frequently reproduced without acknowledgment because the unwary researcher is not aware that what he is copying is a judgment; he fails to distinguish between a judgment and a fact. He must not borrow without acknowledgment such statements as: "Napoleon owed his defeat to the lack of enthusiasm of his troops," or "He owed his defeat to his poorly organized supply lines," or "to his underestimation of Blucher's desire for revenge." These are individual guesses, shaped by the writer's interests and training, as well as his knowledge. Generally, a researcher lacks the specialized training to weigh the factors that defeated Napoleon and decide their relative importance. He must therefore accept the verdicts of those more expert than he, but he must acknowledge that he has done so. The judgments of others, even when stated in the researcher's own words, are best attributed, at least partially, in the text. "According to Col. Liddell-Hart, military historian, Napoleon owed his defeat . . ." That is a partial attribution; the footnote would complete the acknowledgment by citing work and page.

Copying without acknowledgment the judgments of others is most common in treating a literary subject. *"Antigone,"* a student writes, "is the greatest tragedy of Sophocles." How many other plays of Sophocles has he read? What is his definition of a great play? Such pretentious chatter can be avoided by such a simple statement as "Many literary critics have felt that *Antigone* is Sophocles' greatest tragedy." Worse, he may borrow an analogy and write this as his own:

> *Antigone* is a Protestant drama written over four centuries before Christ, for in it Sophocles asserts that we are to regulate spiritual matters, not by church or state authority, but by the dictates of our individual consciences.

Clearly, this is an analogy, a linking together of the thought of Sophocles and the thought of Luther and Calvin, as well as a decision concerning the theme of the play. Both the analogy and the decision are the source's; no student, no matter how impressed with the passage he may be, or how comfortable he finds substituting someone's thinking for his own, has the right to appropriate either. He must acknowledge the source. This is best done partially in the text.

> Dr. Henry Watson, in his *Greek Tragedy and Modern Times*, stresses the concern of Sophocles with the issue that later divided the Western Christian Church, whether we are to obey our individual consciences or bow to the judgments of ecclesiastical and political authorities.

Underdocumentation, then, is a problem, but so may overdocumentation be. Overcautious students overdocument a paper; every sentence may be followed by a footnote numeral. Such a procedure is not only unnecessary, but undesirable. Who wants to read a text when his eye is constantly jerked to the bottom of the page? The simplest rules are these:

1. Document all direct quotations. That may be done wholly in the text, as in the quotation from the Lane biography in the *DNB*, though such a case is rare; or both in the text and in a footnote, as in Haskin's judgment on Waterloo; or solely in a footnote.

2. Document all borrowed opinions, judgments, and analogies. That may be done partially in the text, as in attributing Dr. Watson's analogy of Sophocles and the leaders of the Reformation, and partially in a footnote; or solely in a footnote, if the passage is quoted.

3. Document all conflicting statements. The special form for this is in Appendix II, Footnote and Bibliography Forms.

4. Document facts readers may question, exact figures, precise times, or an odd fact. Suppose that a source states that one of Napoleon's generals failed to support the French attack at Waterloo because he had dreamed that he would be killed, and refused to

march his troops until he had made his will. That must be footnoted, for the anecdote, encountered only in one source, is not widely known and may not be believed.

5. Document all illustrations, maps, graphs, and the like, including those used as a frontispiece.

Now that *what* to footnote is settled, *how* to footnote needs clarification. First, where does the Arabic number that signals a footnote go? At the end of the material accredited, and just above the written or typed line, like this.[1] Some prefer to omit the parentheses.

Does that Arabic number indicate that the sentence before it is borrowed, or a part of that sentence only, or the entire paragraph? That depends.

Patrick Henry shouted, "Give me liberty or give me death!" [1]

No problem here; the footnote documents the quotation.

Rising to his feet, Patrick Henry shouted, "Give me liberty or give me death!" [1]

Reading that and observing the footnote indicator, the reader expects the cited source to contain not only the quoted words, but also the fact that he rose as he spoke. Suppose the source does not mention his rising. Then the sentence can be split.

Patrick Henry rose. He shouted, "Give me liberty or give me death!" [1]

If a paraphrased passage is attributed, the text itself can tell the reader whether the footnote attributes one sentence, two, or a paragraph. Here is such a passage from a paper on the changing social position of actors and actresses in seventeenth-century France.

W. L. Wiley, in his *The Early Public Theatre in France,* states that after 1630 a new breed of actress, educated and intelligent, caused a shift in public opinion. Admired as women, they were not detested as actresses, so that the old stigma of the profession diminished.[1]

The footnote itself may be written at the bottom of the page upon which the attributed material appears, or all footnotes may appear upon a separate sheet at the end of the paper, just before the bibliography.

Some sources may be cited more than once, in which case short footnote forms may be used after the first citation. Suppose we cite W. L. Wiley the first time as follows:

(1) W. L. Wiley, *The Early Public Theatre in France* (Cambridge, 1960), p. 91.

Now follows a second citation from that source. If that second citation is footnote two, that is, *immediately* following footnote one, then we may write:

(2) ibid.

Note the underlining and period. Ibid. is an abbreviation for the Latin *ibidem,* or "in the same place." It is underlined because it is a foreign word. If footnote two cites the same work *and the same page,* then ibid. suffices. If the page is different, that should be indicated.

(2) ibid., p. 132.

Suppose we cite Wiley, then in footnote (2) another book, then in footnote (3) or (5) or (10) Wiley once more. If *The Early Public Theatre in France* is the only work by Wiley in the bibliography, then this short form is used:

(7) Wiley, p. 84.

If Wiley has written more than one work in the paper's bibliography, this short form of both author and title may be used, after its first citation.

(5) Wiley, *Early Public Theatre,* p. 88.

Forms for footnotes are given in Appendix II, Footnote and Bibliography Forms, and in the sample paper. The sample paper footnotes show how to indent them.

5. *The Trimmings:*
Bibliography, Title, and Illustrations

Should a paper's bibliography list every item in the local library, every item read in preparation for the paper, or only every item that was useful? The last. Sources cited in footnotes were obviously useful, and must be listed; a source mentioned in the text but not cited in a footnote must also be listed, as in the case of the biography of Lane, the translator of *The Arabian Nights,* in the *DNB.* Items that were particularly useful for background reading should also be listed, although if they are many, and duplicate each other, a few of these will suffice.

Appendix II, Footnote and Bibliography Forms, will show how to list items in a bibliography as will the bibliography attached to the sample paper. Remember: a thin paper with a thick bibliography is a shanty supported by flying buttresses.

A brief word about the title. It is true that the writer and his instructor will agree upon a title with an academic tone. This agreement is upon the working title, not the title the paper need bear. A student is at liberty to change it to something more attractive if he can, and if he can, he should. The paper on Arabic numerals will not lose its pitch if it is labelled "MCMLXXI to 1971," nor will an instructor groan if "The Contributions of Alchemy to Chemistry" is titled "The Fruits of Greed."

Do not forget to consider illustrating the paper. Now that most libraries have a machine that reproduces a page in a few seconds and for a few cents, illustrations are easy to add, and if none has been encountered in the research, the *Index to Illustration* may unearth one. Such touches as a vivid title and illustrations attract a reader, and they offer visual proof of what the paper asserts.

No one can be taught orally, in class or outside, much that he wants to know. He must be taught to teach himself, and part of that process is to teach him how to consult what exists in print. A library, large or small, embodies what man has pondered and decided to preserve. Books are our intellectual safety deposit box, to which the technique of research provides us a private, individual key. The research paper, then, should not be thought of as just another assignment. Rather, it should be treated as an important step in the liberation and enrichment of the mind.

APPENDICES

Appendix I
BASIC REFERENCE WORKS,
BY SUBJECT

After each work cited, both its Dewey Decimal classification number and its Library of Congress classification number are listed. The Dewey number is preceded by D–; the Library of Congress number is preceded by LC–.

The Cutter number is not given for it is often locally determined and may vary from library to library, particularly in the Dewey system. However, the Cutter number can be guessed. (See the description of how it is assigned in Section II, Chapter 1.)

Bibliographies of Reference Works

1. ALL SUBJECTS

Barton, Mary N., comp. *Reference Books: A Brief Guide for Students and Other Users of the Library.* 6th rev. ed. Baltimore: Enoch Pratt Library, 1966. (D–016; LC–Z1035.1)

Murphey, Robert W. *How and Where to Look It Up.* New York: McGraw-Hill Book Co., 1958. (D–106; LC–Z1035)

Shores, Louis. *Basic Reference Sources.* Chicago: American Library Association, 1954. (D–028.7; LC–Z1035)

Winchell, Constance M. *Guide to Reference Books.* 8th ed. Chicago: American Library Association, 1967. (D–016; LC–Z1035)

2. ART

Lucas, Louise. *Art Books.* Greenwich, Conn.: New York Graphic Society, 1968. (D–016.7; LC–Z5931)
"A basic bibliography on the fine arts."

3. SOCIAL SCIENCES

White, Carl M. *Sources of Information in the Social Sciences.* Totowa, N. J.: Bedminster Press, 1964. (D–106.3: LC–Z7161)

General Encyclopedias

Note below which sets have signed articles, so that you will credit properly in your own bibliography what you take from them. Remember, if the articles are signed by initials, find the full name in the list of contributors.

American People's Encyclopedia. 20 v. New York, 1968. Index; atlas; most articles signed, full name. Alphabetized letter-by-letter. The next step up from the *World Book.* (D–031; LC–AE5)

Collier's Encyclopedia. 24 v. New York, 1962. Index and bibliography in final volume. Major articles signed, full name. Alphabetized letter-by-letter. (D–031; LC–AE5)

Compton's Pictured Encyclopedia and Fact-Index. 15 v. Chicago, 1957. The Fact-Index is split, a section at the end of each volume. Thus volume 1 ("A") contains the index of that volume's contents. Cross-references are frequent. Articles unsigned. Alphabetized letter-by-letter. Many illustrations; easy, concise prose. A set to read when the terminology or background of the subject is strange. (D–031; LC–AG5)

Encyclopedia Americana. 30 v. New York, 1966. Index; major articles signed, full name, with contributor's qualifications. Alphabetized word-by-word. Clear style, excellent articles. (D–031; LC–AE5)

Encyclopaedia Britannica. 24 v. Chicago, 1967. Final volume contains index, bibliography, list of contributors. Major articles signed by initials. Alphabetized letter-by-letter. Scholarly style, usually fullest treatment. Bibliographies often old-fashioned and hard-to-get. Yet this set is indispensable. Note the spelling of both words. (D–030; LC–AE5)

World Book. 20 v. Chicago, 1964. No index. Most articles signed, full name. Alphabetized word-by-word. Articles are short, simple, and aimed at readers with very little knowledge of the subject. (D–031; LC–AE5)

Recommended order of use for a strange subject:

World Book
American People's Encyclopedia
Compton's Pictured Encyclopedia
Collier's Encyclopedia } But Don't Stop Until
Encyclopedia Americana   All Are Read
Encyclopaedia Britannica

Specialized, Yet Wide-ranging Encyclopedias

Encyclopaedia of Religion and Ethics. 13 v. New York, 1955. Index; articles signed, full name. Helpful for most subjects that are not narrowly technical or military. This set is sometimes called "Hastings," its editor's name. Note the spelling of *Encyclopaedia.* (D–203; LC–BL31)

International Encyclopedia of the Social Sciences. 17 v. New York, 1968. Index; rich bibliographies of books and articles; articles signed, full name. Indispensable for economics, sociology, political science, psychology, and the like, as well as history. Articles written for the intelligent layman. (D–300.3; LC–H40.A2)

Jewish Encyclopedia. 12 v. New York, 1916. No index. Jewish faith, history, and lore. Most articles signed, initials. List of contributors in each volume. Useful for the past rather than the present, but what it covers, it covers solidly. (D–296.03; LC–DS102.8)

New Catholic Encyclopedia. 15 v. New York, 1967. Index. Articles signed, full name. Authoritative for Catholic dogma and rites, but also helpful for Catholic view of historic events. Many general articles. (D–282.03; LC–BX841)

New Schaff-Herzog Encyclopedia of Religious Knowledge. 12 v. plus two supplements. Grand Rapids, 1955. Index. Most articles signed, full name. Protestant in tone, but tries to be unbiased. Broader scope than the Catholic and Jewish encyclopedias; not as broad as Hastings. (D–203; LC–BR95)

Shorter Encyclopedia of Islam. Leiden, 1953. Moslem culture, faith, and history. Unsigned. (D–297.03; LC–DS37)

Universal Jewish Encyclopedia. 10 v. New York, 1939. Index. Most articles signed, full name. More emphasis on modern Judaism and Jewish history than its older rival. (D–296.03; LC–DS102.8)

Specialized Reference Works

1. ART

Encyclopedia of World Art. 15 v. New York, 1939. Articles signed, full name. (D–703; LC–N31)

2. BIOGRAPHY

Contemporary Authors. 20 v. Detroit, 1962. All nationalities. (D–928.1; LC–Z1224)

Current Biography. New York, 1940–1967. All nationalities; newsworthy people. (D–920.02; LC–CT100)

Dictionary of American Biography. 22 v. New York, 1943. Indexes. Two supplements. Articles signed, initials. List of contributors in each volume. (D–920.073; LC–E176)

Dictionary of National Biography. 27 v. London, 1937–1959. Supplements.

v. 1–21: from earliest times to 1900	Dictionary form; articles
v. 22: supplement	signed, initials.
v. 23–27: twentieth century, 1901–1950	Articles signed, full name. Index 1901–1930 in v. 25.

An indispensable set. Biographies of British men and women, major and minor. (D–920.042; LC–DA28)

Modern English Biography. 6 v. London, 1965. Index. Articles unsigned. Biographies of English men and women and foreign residents in England who died between 1851 and 1900. (D–920.042; LC–CT773)

National Cyclopedia of American Biography. 61 v. Businessmen, inventors, scientists, professional men, politicians, journalists, and the like. Articles unsigned. This set has *three* indexes; all should be consulted. Many worthies listed whose lives are unavailable elsewhere. Not alphabetically arranged. v. 1–30 to 1944. v. 31–41 from 1944–1956.

v. 42–49 from 1956–1966. Current volumes A–K. A clumsy set, but indispensable. (D–920.073; LC–E176)

New Century Cyclopedia of Names. 3 v. New York, 1954. People, places, and events. Articles unsigned. Worldwide in scope. (D–929.4; LC–PE1625)

3. CLASSIC TIMES: GREEK AND ROMAN

Harper's Dictionary of Classical Literature and Antiquities. New York: American Book Co., 1923. Often the fullest account. Articles unsigned. (D–913.38; LC–DE5)

New Century Classical Handbook. New York, 1962. Articles unsigned. (D–913.38; LC–DE5)

Oxford Companion to Classical Literature. New York, 1962. Desk-size, most useful. Good background articles on history, politics, drama, as well as specifics. Articles unsigned. (D–880.3; LC–DE5)

Sandys, Sir John, ed. *A Companion to Latin Studies.* New York: Hafner Publishing Company, 1968. Background material. Customs, law, education, dress, transport, government, and the like. Excellent. (D–937; LC–DG77)

Whibley, Yeoman. *A Companion to Greek Studies.* 4th rev. ed. New York: Hafner Publishing Company, 1963. Companion to Sandys. (D–913.38; LC–DF77)

4. HISTORY, WORLD

Cambridge Ancient History. 12 v., 5 v. plates. Cambridge, England, 1923–1939. (D–930; LC–D57)

Cambridge Medieval History. 8 v., Cambridge, England, 1911–1936. (D–940.1; LC–D117)

New Cambridge Modern History. 12 v. Cambridge, England, 1968. (D–940.2; LC–D208)

5. HISTORY, AMERICAN

Album of American History. 6 v. New York, 1944. Index. Excellent illustrations. Transport, architecture, political campaigns, as well as economic history. Articles unsigned. (D–973.084; LC–E178)

Dictionary of American History. 6 v. plus index volume. New York, 1946. One volume is a supplement, not indexed. Articles signed, full name. (D–973.03; LC–E174)

Guide to the Study of the United States of America. Washington, D.C.: Library of Congress, 1960. "Representing Books Reflecting the Development of American Life and Thought." A most important source, with an index. Describes the subject matter of thousands of books on every phase of American life and thought. (D–016.9173; LC–Z1215)

Harper's Encyclopedia of United States History. 10 v. New York: Harper and Brothers, 1905. Articles unsigned. Old-fashioned, leisurely account of political and military history. (D–973.03; LC–E174)

Hodge, Frederick W., ed. *Handbook of American Indians North of Mexico.* 2 v. New York: Pageant Books, 1959. Major articles signed, initials. (D–970.1; LC–E77)

Oxford Companion to American History. New York, 1966. Articles unsigned. (D–973.03; LC–E176)

6. HISTORY, CANADIAN

Oxford Companion to Canadian History and Literature. New York, 1967. Useful for U. S. History and literature, as well. Articles unsigned. (D–810.3; LC–PR9106)

7. LITERATURE, AMERICAN

Cambridge History of American Literature. 4 v. New York, 1917–1921. Chapters signed, full name. (D–810.9; LC–PS98)

Guide to the Study of the United States. Washington, D.C., 1960. See entry under American History. (D–016.9173; LC–Z1215)

Hubbell, Jay. *The South in American Literature, 1607–1900.* Durham, N. C., 1954. (D–810.9; LC–PS261)

Oxford Companion to American Literature. New York, 1965. Articles unsigned. (D–810.3; LC–PS21)

Spiller, Robert E., ed., and others. *Literary History of the United States.* 2 v. 3rd rev. ed. New York: The Macmillan Co., 1962–1963. One volume is the history, the other, published in 1962, the bibliographical and supplementary material. Chapters in v. 1 unsigned, but authorship given on pp. 1442–1445. (D–810.9; LC–PS88)

8. LITERATURE, CANADIAN

Oxford Companion to Canadian History and Literature. New York, 1967. Useful for American literature as well. Articles unsigned. (D–810.3; LC–PR9106)

9. LITERATURE, ENGLISH

Cambridge History of English Literature. 15 v. New York, 1939. Index. Chapters signed. (D–820.9; LC–PR83)

New Century Handbook of English Literature. New York, 1967. Articles unsigned. (D–820.3; LC–PR19)

Oxford Companion to English Literature. 4th ed. New York, 1967. Articles unsigned. (D–820.3; LC–PR19)

10. LITERATURE, FRENCH

Oxford Companion to French Literature. New York, 1959. Articles unsigned. (D–840.3; LC–PQ41)

11. SPECIAL LITERARY HELPS

Bartlett's Familiar Quotations. Boston, 1955. When the saying is known, but not the author. Indexed by key words. (D–808.88; LC–PN6081)

Granger's Index to Poetry. 5th ed. New York: Columbia University Press, 1962. When the first line or the title is known, but not the author. (D–808.81; LC–PN4205)

Kuntz, Joseph M. *Poetry Explication.* Rev. ed. Denver: Swallow Press, 1962. Explanations of poems, modern and traditional, by contemporary critics. (D–016.82109; LC–Z2014)

Walker, Warren S. *Twentieth-Century Short Story Explication.* 2nd ed. Hamden, Conn.: Shoe String Press, 1967. (D–016.8093; LC–Z5917) "Interpretations, 1900–1966, and Short Fiction Since 1810."

12. MUSIC

Grove's Dictionary of Music and Musicians. 10 v. New York, 1955. Articles signed, initials. List of contributors in v. 1. (D–780.3; LC–ML100)

International Cyclopedia of Music and Musicians. New York, 1964. (D–780.3; LC–ML100)

Oxford Companion to Music. New York, 1960. Articles unsigned. (D–780.3; LC–ML100)

13. SCIENCE

McGraw-Hill Encyclopedia of Science and Technology. 15 v. New York, 1966. (D–503; LC–Q121)

Sarton, George. *Introduction to the History of Science.* 5 v. Baltimore: Carnegie Institute of Washington, 1927. Scientific thought and experiment from earliest times through the 14th century. General index v. 3. (D–509; LC–Q125)

Singer, Charles and E. J. Holmyard. *A History of Technology.* 5 v. Oxford, 1954. Excellent for the history of the use of materials, techniques. Chapters signed. (D–609; LC–T15)

Thorndike, Lynn. *A History of Magic and Experimental Science.* 8 v. New York: Columbia University Press, 1923–1958. From earliest times through the 17th century. Separate index in v. 4 for v. 1–4; index in v. 6 for 5 and 6; in v. 8 for 7 and 8. (D–509; LC–Q215)

Van Nostrand's Scientific Encyclopedia. Princeton, N. J., 1968. Simple explanations, dictionary form. Rather like *Columbia Encyclopedia.* (D–503; LC–Q121)

14. SPORTS

Menke, Frank G. *The Encyclopedia of Sports.* New York: A. S. Barnes, 1953. (D–796.03; LC–GV11)

15. THEATRE

Oxford Companion to the Theatre. New York, 1967. Some articles signed. (D–792.03; LC–PN2035)

16. MISCELLANEOUS

Illustration Index. 2nd ed. New York: Scarecrow Press, 1966. Useful as a quick key to texts as well as pictures. Indexes books and periodicals. (D–741.6; LC–NC996)

Kane, Joseph N. *Famous First Facts.* New York: H. W. Wilson Co., 1964. Answers "who or what was the first" questions, mostly modern and American. (D–031; LC–AG5)

Library of Original Sources. 10 v. Milwaukee: University Extension Research Co., 1907. Prints texts of important documents, historical, political, legal, scientific, religious. (D–080; LC–AC1)

New Larned History For Ready Reference Reading and Research. 12 v. Springfield, Mass.: C. A. Nichols Publishing Co., 1922–1924. (D–903; LC–D9) "The actual words of the world's best historians, biographers and specialists."

Rivers of America Series. Some forty books have been published in this series on many of the important rivers of the United States. Each book contains valuable chapters on early history, folklore, Indian tribes that inhabited the region, prominent settlers, and many details concerning commerce. Each book has a valuable bibliography. Anyone researching an American historical subject should consult the series.

Works Progress Administration Guides to U. S. States and Cities. During the thirties, the Federal Writers Project, a subdivision of the Works Progress Administration, supervised the writing of a guide to each of the mainland states and some cities. These guides are mines of information on local history, folklore, customs, and the like. In the card catalog they are listed together under *Federal Writers Project,* the *author* entry, or separately under the name of the city or state

followed by the subdivisions *Description and Travel—Guidebooks*.
Like this:

> *Florida—Description and Travel—Guidebooks.*

Indexes

GENERAL

Book Review Digest, 1905–   . Author, subject, title entries.
International Index, 1907–1965. Author, subject entries.
New York Times Index, 1851–   . Subject entry only.
Readers' Guide to Periodical Literature, 1900–   . Author, title, subject
    entries.
Social Sciences and Humanities Index, 1965–   . Author, subject entries.

SPECIALIZED

Agricultural Index, 1916–1964. Subject entry only.
Applied Science & Technology Index, 1958–   . Subject entry only.
Art Index, 1929–   . "Archeology, Architecture, Ceramics, Decoration and
    Ornament, Graphic Arts, Industrial and Applied Design, Landscape
    Architecture, Painting and Sculpture." Author, subject entries.
Biological and Agricultural Index, 1964–   . Subject entry only.
Biography Index, 1946–   . Subject entry only. Indexes both books and
    periodicals; notes portraits.
Book Review Index, 1965–   . Author entry only.
Business Periodicals Index, 1958–   . Subject entry only.
Education Index, 1929–   . Author, subject entries.
Essay and General Literature Index, 1920–   . Author, subject entries, and
    "such title entries as have been deemed necessary." All material has
    appeared in book form; much has also been published in periodicals,
    in which case both appearances are listed.
Music Index, 1949–   . Author, subject, proper name entries.

Appendix II
FOOTNOTE AND
BIBLIOGRAPHY FORMS

There are many styles of footnote and bibliography entries, some simple, some complex. All perform the same function, to send the reader as quickly as possible to the cited source. This manual's forms present few quirks. Basically, breaks in the bibliography entry take periods; in the footnote entry, commas.

Publisher's names are omitted in all footnote forms in this manual, but they are listed in the bibliographic forms, with one exception. When the work is a current and well-known reference work, the publisher's name is omitted.

The footnote form and the bibliography form for each sort of source are listed together. The footnote form is flagged *F*, the bibliography form *B*.

Books

1. BOOK, ONE AUTHOR

F. Chad Walsh, *Doors Into Poetry,* 2nd ed. (Englewood Cliffs, N.J., 1970), p. 103.

B. Walsh, Chad. *Doors Into Poetry.* 2nd ed. Englewood Cliffs, N.J.: Prentice-Hall, Inc., 1970.

2. BOOK, TWO AUTHORS

F.   Roger Sherman Loomis and Rudolph Willard, *Medieval English Verse and Prose* (New York, 1948), p. 430.

B.   Loomis, Roger Sherman and Rudolph Willard. *Medieval English Verse and Prose*. New York: Appleton-Century-Crofts, Inc., 1948.

3. BOOK, MORE THAN TWO AUTHORS

F.   John Rowell Alexander and others, *Signs of Our Times* (New York, 1963), p. 421.

B.   Alexander, John Rowell and others. *Signs of Our Times*. New York: Alfred A. Knopf, 1963.

4. BOOK, EDITED

F.   J. V. Cunningham, ed., *The Renaissance in England* (New York, 1957), p. 18.

B.   Cunningham, J. V., ed. *The Renaissance in England*. New York: The Macmillan Co., 1957.

5. BOOK, MORE THAN ONE VOLUME

F.   Tracy Daugherty, *Matter Versus Mind* (London, 1962), II, p. 407.

B.   Daugherty, Tracy. *Matter Versus Mind*. II v. London: Chatto & Windus, 1962.

6. SIGNED ARTICLE IN A COLLECTION

F.   Carey McWilliams, "California Pastoral," *A Casebook on the Grapes of Wrath*, ed. Agnes McNeil Donohue (New York, 1968), p. 64.

B.   McWilliams, Carey. "California Pastoral." *A Casebook on the Grapes of Wrath*, ed. Agnes McNeill Donohue. New York: T. Y. Crowell Co., 1968.

Encyclopedia Articles

Note: If the article is signed with initials, remember to seek the full name in the List of Contributors.

1. SIGNED

F. James A. Thompson, "Allan, Frederick W." *Dictionary of American Biography,* I, pp. 342–3.

B. Thompson, James A. "Allan, Frederick W." *Dictionary of American Biography,* I. New York, 1958.

2. UNSIGNED

F. "Waterloo, Battle of," *New Century Cyclopedia of Names,* v. 3, p. 4082.

B. "Waterloo, Battle of." *New Century Cyclopedia of Names,* v. 3. New York, 1954.

Magazine Articles

F. S. G. Streshinsky, "Does It Run In The Family?" *Parents Magazine,* 41 (November, 1966), p. 62.

B. Streshinsky, S. G. "Does It Run In The Family?" *Parents Magazine,* v. 41. November, 1966, pp. 60–67. (Note the page span is given.)

Newspaper Articles

F. *The Florida Times-Union,* 17 Feb., 1969, p. 3.

B. *Florida Times-Union, The.* 17 Feb., 1969, p. 3.

Special Footnotes

CONTRADICTIONS

While one source suggests that the original Kensington Stone is in Minnesota and the copy in the National Museum in Washington, another states the exact reverse.[1]

(1) William G. Bark, "Kensington Rune Stone," *World Book* (1964), *K*, p. 214; Karl E. Schonfelt, *North American Runes* (Chicago, 1927), p. 109.

SECOND CITINGS IN FOOTNOTES

After the first reference to a source, most instructors permit a shorter form for subsequent citings. Thus Chad Walsh, *Doors Into Poetry*, once cited, could be shortened. If Walsh has written only one entry in the bibliography, we can, *after the first full citing*, write:

(3) Walsh, p. 174.

If Walsh has written more than one entry in the bibliography, we must include the title, either in full or shortened form.

(3) Walsh, *Doors Into Poetry*, p. 174.

WARNING: Ibid. is both a foreign word and an abbreviation. A period must therefore always follow it, to signal the abbreviation, and it must be underlined, as a foreign word. It means "in the same place," and can refer only to the note that immediately precedes it. Better to avoid it, and use the short, second citing form.

Roman Numerals

I	—	1
V	—	5
X	—	10
L	—	50
C	—	100
D	—	500
M	—	1,000
MCM	—	1,900

A line drawn over a letter means "thousands." Hence, $\overline{V}$ is 5,000.

Appendix III
SAMPLE PAPER

How the Greek Trilogies

Were Financed

Elliot Hindman
Winter Term
C. P. Lee
English 111, Section 12

1.

Anyone who buys a ticket for a Broadway play knows his motive. He wants entertainment. He also knows one motive of the organizers of the play. Its playwright and producer may want to create an artistic experience, they may want personal fame, but they certainly hope for cash. Whether the plays these motives breed will last we do not know. What we do know is that the Greek tragedies, believed by some the greatest Western plays, were shaped by motives different from ours. The Greek spectator who went to see Antigone or Oedipus Rex may have been entertained, but he went to the play as a religious duty. The Greek producer, far from hoping to make money, knew that he would lose it. Why were the Greek tragedies produced, and how were they financed?

The ancient Greeks enjoyed one of the most advanced civilizations the Mediterranean world had ever witnessed. Those Greeks who were religious attributed the cultural heights and affluence they enjoyed to the gods. Those who were not religious were content to join in the praise. To pay homage to those gods, elaborate and extensive religious festivals were organized, of which theatrical performances constituted a major part. Because these plays were religious performances, state acts of homage to the state's gods, the dramatic performances were organized by the state. Around 534 B.C., Pisistratus, tyrant of Athens, inaugurated the festival of Dionysus, the most important of the Greek religious festivals, at which Thespis, widely accepted as the

2.
(1)

founder of Greek tragedy, won the first Athenian tragic contest.
The organization of this festival and its dramatic competition
were copied almost exactly in many other festivals throughout
Greece.

Plays for the festivals were selected by state authorities,
who controlled all theatrical activities as well as all other
arrangements for the festivals. These authorities would select
from applicants the poets allowed to compete, usually three for
tragedy and five for comedy. To have a play accepted for competition was a great honor in itself. Whether scripts of plays
were submitted, or whether the committee chose poets rather than
plays is not clear. H. D. F. Kitto mentions that Aristophanes
must have injected certain topical references immediately before
the performance, and conjectures that probably well-known poets
were allowed to submit "scenarios", while lesser-known poets had
(2)
to submit scripts.

Ten judges of the plays were selected from the citizens,
some by election, some by appointment. These ten sat in seats of
honor in the front rows of the theater, and at the conclusion of
the performances placed their votes for the

---

(1)
    Margarete Bieber, The History of the Greek and Roman
Theater (Princeton, N. J., 1961), p. 19; H. D. F. Kitto, "Thespis,"
Oxford Companion to the Theater (New York, 1967), p. 945.

    (2)H. D. F. Kitto, "Greece," Oxford Companion to the Theater
p. 407.

Footnote (1) represents a simple way to document a statement
which incorporates material from two sources. Part of the material
in the flagged sentence—that Pisistratus inaugurated the festival in
about 534 B. C.—comes from Bieber, but the information that this
festival marked the first Athenian tragic contest is from Kitto.
Rather than split this sentence and footnote each one, this writer
preferred to use this double footnote. Note that this form may also
be used for a contradiction, as in footnote (16).

3.

best poet in an urn. Only five of these votes were withdrawn
from the urn, and the majority of these decided the competition.
The best poet was announced. "The winning poet was brought to
the stage and crowned with a chaplet of ivy, a solemn sacrifice
was made, and the proceedings wound up with a grand banquet given
by the poet to his actors, chorus and friends." (3) In later
times, the second-best poet was also announced, and Kitto says
that prizes were awarded to all three competing poets. During
the fifth century a play could not be repeated in Athens, except
the plays of Aeschylus, for whom an exception was made, and his
plays were frequently revived. Plays successful in Athens were
staged outside that city. (4)

The theater itself was constructed by the state and was its
property. Some authorities mention that under certain circumstances it could be leased by citizens for special occasions. The
plays selected, the producer was named. Modern playwrights may
produce their own plays, although they seldom do. In ancient
Greece they were forbidden to do so. The state appointed an
official known as a _choregus_ to produce each poet's work. This
man was tapped from the state's list of wealthy citizens, a list
of rich men who could be called upon at any time for such civic

---

(3)
    James Cleaver, _Theatre Through the Ages_ (New York, 1967),
p. 27.
    (4)
    Kitto, "Greece," p. 407.

Footnote (4) is the short form, because the full documentation
has been given in footnote (2).

4.

duties as equipping a warship, paying for a state delegation's
visit to Delphi, or producing a play.[5]   He was chosen for the
task by lot. Perhaps there were two reasons for this method.
The more practical is that a stingy <u>choregus</u> might skimp on
costumes or props and endanger the quality of the production.
Poets assigned a stingy <u>choregus</u> might justly complain; therefore
the selection by lot. Another reason may be that the gods could
be considered 'as expressing their will in the lot, as in the
withdrawing from the urn of only five of the judges' votes.
Stingy <u>choregi</u> were rare after the state began the practice of
honoring the <u>choregus</u> of the winning production as well as the
poet. After that the <u>choregi</u> went to great lengths to buy the
best actors and the best costumes. Upon occasion they went to
such an extreme in their quest that they found themselves finan-
cially ruined. Despite the expense, some must have served frequently; Ninias and Christisthenes are recorded as lavish
<u>choregi</u> who with their poets won honors in many festivals.[6]
The quest for the best chorus encouraged professionals to form
guilds of players who travelled all over the Hellenistic world,
attracted from one post to another by the offer of a better wage.

   The <u>choregus</u> had many expenses. He had to provide a teacher

---

[5]
   <u>Ibid.</u>
[6]
   Cleaver, p. 27.

Footnote (5) shows the shortest possible form, when the source
and page of the preceding footnote are the same.

5.

who taught the songs and dances to the chorus, had to provide
the chorus accommodations, and "such meat and drink as would
contribute to strengthen their voices."[7]   He had to provide
suppers, props and costumes, and most authorities state that he
had to pay the actors and chorus as well. However, Kitto states
that the state itself paid for the three chief actors for a
tragedy and the chorus, and the _choregus_ paid everything else.[8]
Probably this is a concession made as Athens weakened economically.
During the Peloponnesian War, times were hard, and the state permitted the expenses of a production to be shared by two or more
choregi, and by the end of the fourth century B.C. the state had
been forced to assume all costs.[9]

No matter how much a _choregus_ spent on the production, if
he won he had to spend more, for his prize was a tripod which had
to be consecrated, and for that consecration he had to pay. Often
he had to pay for the monument on which the tripod was mounted,
to be publicly exhibited. In Athens, a Street of the Tripods
existed, lined with such monuments.[10]

---

[7]
    "Choregus," _Harper's Dictionary of Classical Literature
and Antiquities_, p. 335.
[8]
    Kitto, "Greece," p. 407.
[9]
    Cleaver, p. 29.
[10]
    "Choregus," p. 335.

6.

At first all performances were free, but several problems arose. Many people would come to the theater the day before the performance, take the best seats, and spend the night to keep them. Also many foreigners occupied a large portion of the seats. Therefore, the state initiated the issuing of tickets for seats and a small charge. The price of admission for a one-day performance was two obols, for a three-day dramatic program, one drachma.(11) Tickets still exist, of lead and ivory, with pictures on them of a theater, or even the name of the poet and play to be performed. Presumably the lead markers admitted to the general auditorium, the ivory to reserved seats.(12) Everyone, including prisoners, was entitled to see the performances, as they were part of a sacred festival, and everyone had to be admitted, whether he had money or not. Therefore, for the citizen too destitute to afford the fee, the state provided the cost. Pericles, who ruled Athens from 461 B.C. to 429 B.C., provided all needy citizens with the price of admission and also compensated them for the time lost in attendance.(13)

---

(11)
    Karl Mantzius, <u>A</u> <u>History</u> <u>of</u> <u>Theatrical</u> <u>Art</u> <u>in</u> <u>Ancient</u> <u>and</u> <u>Modern</u> <u>Times</u> (New York, 1937), v. I, p. 149.
(12)
    <u>Ibid</u>.
(13)
    Julius Bab, "Theater," <u>Encyclopedia</u> <u>of</u> <u>the</u> <u>Social</u> <u>Sciences</u> (1934), v. XIV, p. 601.

Footnote (13) shows the copyright date of the *Encyclopedia of Social Sciences*. It should do so because the edition used is out-of-date, and a reader lacking that copyright date would, without turning to the bibliography, seek the information in the current set. Needless to say, he would not find it.

7.

Plays were central portions of two Athenian festivals, the
Lenaea and the City Dionysia. Comedies were performed at both,
but tragedies only in the latter, held in the spring. The City
Dionysia lasted five or six days, but only three days were
devoted to drama. The first day an elaborately costumed pro-
cession wound through the streets to bring a statue of the god
Dionysus to the theater and "set it up in state." [14]   On the
actual day of the performance, the poet himself announced the
plays to be performed. Three tragedies and a satyr play were
performed. The audience sat on stone benches from dawn to dusk,
with only one break. They were, however, well behaved. James
Cleaver, in his Theatre Through the Ages states: "All citizens
were expected to be on their best behavior, any offences committed
during this period being punished severely and the offenders
publicly castigated at the close of the festival." [15]   Judges
and honored guests sat in the front rows; men sat separately from
women, probably at the back. Slaves who had their masters' permission also were permitted to attend. How large the audience
was is a matter of debate. Estimates of the size of the audience

---

[14]
    Cleaver, p. 26. However, the author of "Choregus" in
Harper's Dictionary of Classical Literature and Antiquities states
that "an old wooden statue of Dionysus. . . was borne. . . to a
small temple in the neighborhood of the Acropolis and back again."
    [15]
    Cleaver, p. 30.

Footnote (14) shows another way of stating a contradiction. The
dissenting authority's view is stated textually, and the documentation follows. This form is best used when one authority disputes several others. No further documentation is needed, for the "Choregus"
article has been fully cited in footnote (7), and the article is short.

8.

(16)
vary from seventeen thousand to thirty thousand.

The fifth and perhaps a sixth day of the festival was devoted to the award of special civic honors and to a choral contest between regional societies, the Greek equivalent of our glee clubs.

This lavishness of the state contributed to the rise of the Greek drama. Without this state aid, without this scrupulous care to produce the scripts as impressively as possible, no poet would have dared to write dramas with the sweep of <u>Antigone</u> and <u>Oedipus Rex</u>, dramas we cherish today.

---

(16)
    Cleaver, p. 42; Mantzius, p. 150.

Footnote (16) shows the form for a contradiction when two authorities disagree. The shortened form is used because both sources have been fully cited before.

112 APPENDIX III

9.

BIBLIOGRAPHY

Bab, Julius. "Theater," Encyclopedia of the Social Sciences
    (1934), XIV.

Bieber, Margarete. History of the Greek and Roman Theater.
    Princeton, N. J.: Princeton University Press, 1939.

Cleaver, James. Theater Through the Ages. New York City: Hart
    Publishing Company, Inc., 1967.

Flickinger, Roy Cason. The Greek Theater and Its Drama. Chicago:
    University of Chicago Press, 1936.

Hartnoll, Phyllis, ed. The Oxford Companion to the Theater,
    Third edition. New York: Oxford University Press, 1967.

Mantzius, Karl. A History of Theatrical Art in Ancient and
    Modern Times, VI v. New York: Peter Smith, 1937.

Peck, Harry Thurston, ed. Harper's Dictionary of Classical
    Literature and Antiquities. New York: American Book Company,
    1923.

INDEX

E

Education Index, 48, 62
Encyclopaedia Britannica, 34, 35, 36, 38, 56, 59
Encyclopaedia of Religion and Ethics (Hastings), 13–14, 19, 37, 57
Encyclopedia Americana, 34, 35, 44
Encyclopedia of European Literature, 41
Encyclopedia of World Art, 41, 59
Encyclopedia of World Literature, 41
Encyclopedias, 34–41 (*see also* Reference works and Appendix I)
  alphabetizing in, 35–36
  editions of, 36
  entries for, on bibliography cards, 18
  special sets, 36–41
  use of, 34–35
Essay and General Literature Index, 48–49, 61, 62

F

Famous First Facts (Kane), 56, 58
Footnotes, 77–82 (*see also* Appendix II)
  borrowed opinions, documentation of, 80
  conflicting statements, 80
  direct quotations, 80
  facts, 80
  form of citation, 81–82
  illustrations, documentation of, 81
  numbers, placement of, 81

G

Grove's Dictionary of Music and Musicians, 61
Guide to Reference Books (Winchell), 41

H

Handbook of American Indians North of Mexico, 39–40, 55, 57
Harper's Cyclopedia of American History, 39